Lenore RS Lim
Layered Life A
Mixed Media, 2015
30" x 24"

Don't Forget the Parsley

And More from
My Positively Filipino Family

Christmas 2015

Don't Forget the Parsley

And More from
My Positively Filipino Family

Marie Claire Lim Moore

PROMONTORY
P R E S S

Copyright © 2016 by Marie Claire Lim Moore

ALL RIGHTS RESERVED.
No part of this book may be reproduced or transmitted in any form by any
means, electronic or mechanical, including photocopying and recording, or
by any information storage and retrieval system, except as may be expressly
permitted in writing from the publisher or the author.

Published by
Promontory Press
1628 Dean Park Road, North Saanich, BC, Canada V8L 4Y7

Library of Congress Cataloging-in-Publication Data
Lim Moore, Marie Claire.
Don't Forget the Parsley (And More from My Positively Filipino Family)
Marie Claire Lim Moore
p.   cm.

ISBN° 978–1–987857–51–1 (paperback)
ISBN° 978–1–987857–52–8 (ebook)

PRINTED IN THE PHILIPPINES
CGKFORMAPRINT
CGK Building, 2275 P. Burgos St., Pasay City, 1300
Metro Manila, Philippines

Book design and layout: Nonie Cartagena-dono
Prints: Lenore RS Lim

For my parents, Jose and Lenore, my loves, Alex, Carlos, Isabel and Sofia, and my brother Justin

TABLE OF CONTENTS

Family trip to Vancouver Island in 1982

Introduction

Interview with Howie Severino on *GMA News to Go*

WHY I WROTE THIS BOOK

ONE THING I LEARNED SHORTLY after writing my first book is that inevitably people will be asking about your next one. I didn't necessarily plan on doing a follow up but I was certainly encouraged by all the support.

Don't Forget the Soap is a collection of anecdotes from my family's global journey starting with my parents' migration from the Philippines to my current experiences living abroad with my husband and our then two children. I would be lying if I said my heart didn't burst the first time I saw the book featured in *People Asia* on the same "Papertrail" page as Malala Yousafazi's *I Am Malala*. Or that my relatives didn't take about a gazillion selfies with our family memoir sitting on the same "New & Hot Non-Fiction" shelf as Hillary Clinton's *Hard Choices*. Or that we weren't glued to our smartphones refreshing Amazon until we saw the book climb to #1 Hot New Release in it-didn't-matter-what category.

While the book tours, talk shows, and photo shoots have been fabulously unexpected, equally fun has been meeting people from all different walks of life who have come to admire my parents (almost) as much as I do.

I always figured that Filipinos and Filipino-Americans would relate to the SPAM and corned beef references, but I've been delightfully surprised to learn how much the book has resonated with so many different people. Whether their courage to leave a comfortable life (from Manila to Mobile, Alabama, to Vancouver, Canada, to New York City), their parenting techniques ("you're too smart to be bored"), or their practical approach to life (wow… appetizers!), people seemed to connect to my parents (and my family) more than I ever imagined. The following is a list of my beloved readership so far.

- Filipinos and Filipinos abroad (okay, no surprise here);
- Anyone with Filipino friends or in-laws: those who have somehow found themselves amidst the Filipino

experience, wondering why they are being egged on (no pun intended) to eat a fertilized duck embryo[1], kissing more *Titas* than they know what to do with, and going to church more often than they thought physically possible;

- Asian-Americans and other immigrants: it turns out all these ethnic groups have relatives who stay with them for months at a time;
- Europeans, Latin Americans, Africans, and basically anyone who feels close to their family: it didn't seem like it while I was younger, but a lot of people enjoy spending time with their parents and siblings;
- Women trying to balance it all: I didn't realize I was speaking to this audience as I was writing the book but they have turned out to be some of my greatest supporters.

Don't Forget the Soap has been coined everything from a "happy family handbook" to a "great big hug in a book" but I wasn't purposely going for that. There are a number of books like *The Happiness Project* or *Stumbling on Happiness* that methodically try to measure and dissect happiness. I just wanted to share stories about my family while recounting lessons from my mother. I guess I could have anticipated the result. For as long as I can remember, someone was always commenting on our happy disposition.

One day in college, I was logging into email on my friend Nic's computer. Electronic mail was in its infancy stage and Yale was using an old system called Minerva, which had a series of codes you needed to enter into the DOS screen before your password. Back then, the DOS system cursor could not always keep up with fast a person typed. My rhythm must have been off because somehow my password displayed up on the screen in what was supposed to be an innocuous field.

---

[1] Balut is an infamous Philippine delicacy, which was once even featured in the TV show *Fear Factor*

Morning breakfast in temporary housing during our recent move to Hong Kong

"Aww… is that really your password?" Nic asked, chuckling. He was referring to the letters I had just typed on the screen: S-M-I-L-E.

"Yes, but why are you laughing?"

"It's just that I've always wondered if you're as happy as you seem, or if it's just an act, and now I know the answer," he explained nonchalantly as he put in the new Notorious B.I.G. CD. I didn't know whether to be offended that he doubted my sincerity or whether to appreciate his.

My husband, Alex, had a similar first impression. We met in Sao Paulo, Brazil, while we were both working there as management associates with Citibank. There was an instant chemistry between us from the start, but for the first three months he thought I was being disingenuous half the time. "Who is *that* bubbly twenty-four hours a day?" I remember him skeptically saying. It wasn't until my family came to visit over Christmas when he had the realization, "Well, I guess *they* are …" And the rest is history.

In general, Filipinos are a happy bunch. Survey after survey and year after year, the Philippines comes up on top of every happiness index from *The Economist* to Instagram. This is one of the reasons why the country's recent tourism tagline, "It's more fun in the Philippines," couldn't be more perfect. Launched in 2012 to attract visitors to the country, this campaign has been incredibly successful in creating positive buzz. In fact, marketing intelligence service Warc released its annual Warc 100 list of the world's top marketing campaigns and ranked this campaign as third, behind only Vodafone's Fakka (Egypt) and American Express' Small Business Saturday (USA). Using Filipinos themselves as the inspiration for the campaign and slogan was pure genius.

Beyond the seemingly inherent Filipino trait, however, I attribute our happiness to my parents from whom I've learned nearly everything. My mother has taught me how to stock a pantry so you're always visitor ready, how to perfectly wrap a gift, and how to properly greet my elders. My father has taught me how to drive a stick shift on the hills of Sao Paulo, how to talk to anyone about anything, and how to efficiently pack a *balikbayan* box. Both of them have taught me how to be kind, thankful, and patient. But, the most important lesson I've learned from them is this: the happiest people don't *have* the best of everything—they *make* the best of everything.

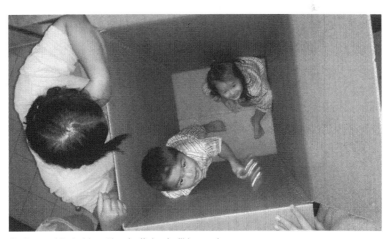

Carlos and Isabel in a "jumbo" size balikbayan box

Morning breakfast prepared by my mother when we were kids

It wasn't long ago that my parents immigrated to North America with everything they owned in two suitcases. They lived in a one-bedroom basement suite, my mother worked as a Reitmans department store clerk while my father took a side job at Pizza Patio. They held birthday parties for my brother and me in the playland at a nearby McDonald's. Now they jet set around the world, have a comfortable home base in the heart of three global cities, and leisurely spend their days surrounded by family and friends.

I'm not saying life is perfect. "This isn't heaven," my mother always reminds me when I'm frustrated that something didn't work out the way I wanted. Like everyone else, my parents have their share of challenges and bumps in the road, but somehow they always find a constructive way to deal with them. They manage to turn around any tough situation by finding the positive in it. They do this for everything, big and small.

A few months ago, as my parents were preparing to leave for the airport there was an overall rush and nervous energy in our Singapore apartment. My father was trying to figure out how to print their boarding passes on our antiquated printer, my mother was walking me through how she had reorganized the kids'

An expert traveler at age 3

drawers, and Alex was loading the car with their suitcases. Trying to be helpful, my four-year-old son Carlos turned off the air conditioner in his bedroom while we were getting ready to leave the apartment. He must have missed the shelf as he was putting down the remote control because it fell with a loud bang. I ran over to see what had happened.

"Oh no!" I exclaimed. Not only was there a crack in the screen but the digital display was also broken. It wasn't the end of the world but it was the last air conditioner remote in the apartment that worked (air conditioning is crucial in Singapore). Of course, I wasn't angry with Carlos but I was noticeably annoyed. "This is going to be a pain. I have no idea where to get another one of these things and the landlord will probably charge us a boatload. How are we going to tell the temperature in the meantime?" I was muttering under my breath.

"It's okay," my mother reminded me. "It can be replaced. Better the controller have a bad fall than one of the kids. Be thankful that this was the bump for the day." And just like that, the broken air conditioner remote became the best thing in the world.

"Making the best of everything" encapsulates what I love most about my parents. It also summarizes their immigrant experience as well as our family existence. It has been so engrained in me that I subconsciously apply it to my own personal and professional life. When I realized that I could probably write another book solely on how my parents lived out this mantra, I decided to go for it. This book attempts to answer the recurring question, "How are you guys always this happy?" It comes down to living your best life, enjoying every moment, and remembering the little things.

Many people thought my parents were crazy when they decided to pick up and relocate to New York City in their early forties. As first-generation immigrants to Vancouver, Canada, they were just finally getting comfortable when they decided to make the big move. My father was building a strong reputation as a financial advisor at Eaton Bay Financial Services; my mother had started a successful preschool at Our Lady of Lourdes, a Catholic school two blocks from our home. They were both highly regarded in the local community. No one could understand why on earth they would want to disrupt their stable lives.

The fact that they had two young children and limited income did not deter them from moving to New York City because they were incredibly resourceful. Through one of her former colleagues from International School Manila, my mother learned of an opening at the United Nations International School (UNIS). She secured this highly sought-after job, which meant that my brother and I could attend the prestigious private school at no cost. After getting his real estate license, my father familiarized himself with Manhattan housing and secured us one of the limited spots at Waterside Plaza, which was part of the Mitchell-Lama Housing Program that developed affordable housing for middle income residents. It also happened to be located right next to UNIS so it couldn't have been any more convenient for our family.

Beyond housing and schools, my parents also managed to sprinkle unique experiences throughout each year, which also added color to our lives. We went to Broadway shows because my mother found a way to get $10 tickets for the back row. Sure, we were next to people who were using their seats at *CATS* to eat Chinese take-out but it didn't matter. My mother and I were able to go on a mother-daughter trip to Italy and stay at an old convent because of my parents' involvement with the Christian Life Community. My father and brother Justin traveled to France together after my brother got a music scholarship in Provence. Their ingenuity also helped me find an international student scholarship to Yale.

Now that I have a family of my own, I often find myself reflecting on my own past, my own childhood, and everything I've learned from my parents. In some ways, my kids are growing up under completely different circumstances. While I had the immigrant experience, my children are having the expat experience. My son just turned five and he has already lived in New York City, Singapore, and now Hong Kong. My two-and-a-half-year-old daughter likes San Pellegrino sparkling water and French cheese, and my nine month old has been globetrotting since the womb. Regardless of how much or how little they have, one of the most important lessons I can teach my children is how to live their best life. During a recent interview, someone asked me what kind of legacy I wanted to leave behind. That would be it.

One of Justin's most popular Instagram posts

Living your best life is not a novel idea. Google the phrase and you'll see all sorts of headlines, tips, and steps on how to live your full potential. Oprah made this phrase famous, and my dear friend and women's empowerment expert Claudia Chan promotes a similar idea. It's also something my parents have been showing me for as long as I can remember. Like anything learned, however, it's one thing when you're memorizing steps and acronyms, but another when it's simply what you see and know. I'm grateful to my parents for giving me this head start. Living your best life is the best example they could have set for my brother and me.

There are a few more reasons I decided to write another book:

- I remembered many more family anecdotes that I want to share with my kids;
- I've had a lot of requests to share more stories about my dad and my brother (and I aim to please);
- I've had some insights (or at least stray observations) since writing my first book;
- I'm on another maternity leave. When I found out I was pregnant a few months back the first thought that crossed my mind was, *How wonderful! Carlos and Isabel have been so great and now we get to have another!* And I have to admit that my second thought was, *Hmm ... I wonder if I'll have a chance to write another book;*
- "Everybody has one book in them. Almost nobody has two." The other night Alex and I were watching *The Affair*, a new Showtime TV drama series. The main character in this show is a writer made rich by Hollywood movies. When his father-in-law says this as a dig to him, it ended up challenging me.

Here are a few things you may observe since the first book:

1. I still like lists but I have also expanded to litmus tests.
2. I still like footnotes but I use less of them. EBooks don't make footnotes very fun as all the notes are con-

With Consul General Mario De Leon in New York City for the first launch of *Don't Forget the Soap*

solidated at the end of each chapter (as opposed to at the bottom of each page) so I've tried to incorporate most of my side comments into the overall text.

3. I still tell a lot of stories about my mom but I also tell more stories about my dad. Not surprisingly, there has been just as much interest in my father as my mother. As I have mentioned on several occasions, he has been just as influential on my life though it was mother who explicitly verbalized her reminders.

4. I still make a lot of TV and pop culture references.

5. My family remains as corny as ever.

Like the first book, this one is not meant to be prescriptive by any means. If, by taking another trip down memory lane and reflecting on what I've learned, I'm able to give others another perspective they find helpful, then that's fabulous. Otherwise, it is part two of my family memoir that I hope my children at the very least will enjoy.

My father and his colleagues at Eaton Bay Financial in the early eighties

With old college friends, Nicolas King and Carlos Reyes-Hailey at our ten year
Yale reunion

Family photo during Justin's last visit to Singapore

Sibling laughter and love

Classic birthday parties   Classic portrait studio photos

One of many photos of family members in front of this bookshelf

Our first arrival to Singapore when we moved from New York in 2011

Relocating to Hong Kong in 2015

Our favorite tagline

Background

Everyday joys

Don't Forget the Parsley

My MOTHER ALWAYS ADDS A TOUCH OF COLOR to every plate before it's served. Usually it's parsley. Sometimes celery leaves. Other times green onions, or whatever bright vegetable is readily available in our refrigerator. Filipino food is delicious but it isn't always the most visually appealing since many of the dishes are stewed or sautéed in a brownish sauce of sorts. Soy sauce, *patis* (fish sauce), and *bagoong* (shrimp paste) make great flavor, but not necessarily great color. For this reason, garnishing the dishes became part of setting the table in our household and our plates always looked restaurant ready.

Recently there has been a rise in Filipino restaurants, particularly in the US. I've been thrilled about this surge since I've often been asked about the lack thereof. Certainly the population of Filipinos is much higher than the number of Thai in the US but you wouldn't know this if number of restaurants were any indication. There are many reasons for this, none of which are, "Filipino food must not be very good ..." as my Mexican-American friends Danny and Joaquin like to tease. They know how much this sets me off and for over a decade now I continue to forward them every article I come across about the gaining popularity of Filipino cuisine.

I wasn't the only Filipino-American who wanted to show the world Filipino food. And there have certainly been others more qualified to do so. The owners of Maharlika and Jeepney in New York City have launched breakthrough Filipino restaurants with these two establishments.[2] They passed the litmus test (would non-Filipinos go to this restaurant?) with flying colors. Justin has even bumped into *Top Chef* host Padma Lakshmi eating with her daughter at Maharlika. They have managed to make the food authentic enough so our parents go there and the venue cool enough so us kids go there (and by kids I mean us twenty-five to forty year olds). They have also figured out how to put a fun spin on their restaurants, coming out with "Tagalog word of the day" on their menu boards, and T-shirts that say, "My best friend is Filipino" and equally popular, "My ex is Filipino." And, sure enough, proper garnishing is a vital part of their dishes.

My second generation cousins and friends often poke fun at many of the staple foods we all used to have in the pantry when we were growing up such as corned beef, SPAM, and Vienna sausage (some of us still have them in our pantry today). But, my mother even prepares these simple dishes in a special way. She sautés the corned beef with garlic and onions, cooks them with fried potatoes, and then serves them on a bed of green lettuce. She could just as well be plating on *Top Chef*. Okay, maybe Filipino *Top Chef*.

"Don't forget the parsley," my mother would often remind us as we helped with dinner. We would then go back to the fridge and decorate each of the Corningware serving plates before laying them out on the table.

---

[2] Please put these on your must-try list for your next trip to NYC.

"You do this even when you don't have company?" I remember my mom's brother *Tito* Francis asking her.

"Of course," my mother would answer with a smile. "Every day should be a special experience, you know. You have to keep life exciting."

Only recently have I come to realize that this simple reminder doesn't only apply to our meals but to all facets of life whether on your plate, at your office, or in your home. "Don't forget the parsley," is just one example of how my mother lives her best life every day.

She would do this at work as well as at home. Teaching at the United Nations International School allowed her to have the same schedule as her kids, it paid the bills, and she was naturally great with children. That said, spending all day with eighteen five-year-old children could be draining at times so she always looked for ways to keep her job exciting by incorporating her true love, art, wherever possible. She also found ways to get involved with aspects of the school where she could utilize her talents.

One way she did this was by joining the UNIS Hospitality Committee. While this may sound about as exciting as paying bills, it gave my mother a surprising amount of satisfaction and fulfillment. One of her proudest achievements was the staff lounge. Before the Hospitality Committee came about, the staff lounge was about as riveting as it sounds. A few classroom tables and chairs were thrown into the center of the room with sagging sofas in one corner, and an old refrigerator and microwave in another; the teachers' lunchroom on *Glee* would have been an upgrade. Teachers would come in quickly to check their mailbox for memorandums (well before email), some would use the microwave to warm up their lunch, and others (mostly English and drama teachers) would use the "smokers' corner" but otherwise no staff would ever be found lounging.

The Hospitality Committee decided to give the staff lounge a makeover. They went to the UNIS administration with a proposal for improvements. My mother was used to making something out of nothing so even a shoestring budget was sufficient—a few hundred dollars at IKEA goes a long way. Once word got around about the effort underway, fellow staff members also began donating other accent pieces. Applying her artistic eye, my mother tastefully arranged all the new and contributed items. Soon, teachers began spending more of their free time in the lounge, conversing with colleagues instead of spending break times alone in their empty classroom. If HGTV had been around then, it could have made a great pilot for *Office Makeover*.

The more often the UNIS staff got together, more collaborative ideas emerged. Some ideas were student focused. In one instance, the French teacher from the Junior School connected with the French teacher from the Middle School about a French mentoring program for students to help each other practice and solidify what they were learning. Other ideas were staff focused, building camaraderie amongst teachers. For example, the PE teachers started offering morning aerobics classes for those interested in exercising together before school started.

The *pièce de résistance* was the rotating art exhibits my mother would curate in the lounge. The UNIS Manhattan campus is located on reclaimed land that overlooks the East River so almost every room in the school, including the staff lounge, has coveted views of the water. It was easy to take this for granted as a student walking into school every day but, as a grownup who understands the cost of New York City real estate, the UNIS location was ridiculously impressive. With its interior facelift and beautiful natural light, my mother came up with the idea of showcasing work of fellow colleagues. When you're a student it's hard to think of your teacher doing anything outside of the classroom so it was amazing to learn how many of them painted, took photos, or wrote poetry. At first, the work on display was by the usual suspects (i.e. paintings by the art teachers). Soon enough, however, even the Director of the school, Dr. Kenneth Wrye, was sharing some of the photographs he had taken in Afghanistan. Something as seemingly minor as the Hospitality Committee or the staff lounge started adding color to so many lives.

My freshman college dorm room decorated in Laura Ashley Bramble

It doesn't matter who you are or what you're doing, you'll be happier if you're living your best life. My parents have recently moved into a new premier condo development in Manila called The Grove by Rockwell, located off the C5 highway near the Marikina River. As my mother was showing me the view from their condo unit, she pointed out one particular home in the middle of a shantytown that we could see from a distance. In the sea of make-shift houses cobbled together from plywood, corrugated metal, and cardboard boxes, I could see bright pink bougainvillea.

I gazed at this house with the bougainvillea and saw the clean shutters, neat wires, and overall maintenance. "That family is making the best of what they have. Those are the people who will most likely be happy and successful," my mother commented. She

Carlos garnishing his dinner plate (he's learned from the best)

Carlos' lunch prepared by Nanny Richel (also trained by my mother)

Using my "birthday half day" to stroll along the beach at Repulse Bay in Hong Kong

knew this from personal experience. "When your father and I were living in the basement suite of a house in Vancouver, it was even more important to keep our space nice and tidy. The less you have, the more you need things to sparkle." It's the same reason she encourages me to dress up when I'm feeling sick or down.

I often think about all the ways we add color to our lives. Sometimes we do it through major life events like moving to a new city or taking a new job. Other times we do little things like make up silly games or recount favorite memories. My publicist, Carissa Villacorta, recently asked me if I could think of five things I do that add finesse to my daily life (she was doing some market research for a rebrand). I was surprised by how quickly I could answer her question. I didn't want to stop at five but I decided to leave a few things for the rest of this book.

Here were the five that came to mind right away:

1. I garnish every meal (my mother trained me well). As mentioned, Filipino food is delicious but a lot of the dishes can have an overall brown coloring. Sliced green onions, hardboiled egg, lemon, and sliced shrimp can significantly enhance the experience.

2. I've become a lady who lunches—a *working* lady who lunches. Throughout the month, I sprinkle fabulous lunches in my calendar. First, it gives me the opportunity to catch up with friends, mentors, mentees, clients, and business partners. Second, it gives me the chance to try out new restaurants without breaking the bank. Time of day factors into how much you spend at restaurants. If you want to try out a celebrity chef restaurant, go there for lunch. You'll get pretty much the same experience and a good taste of what it offers without the expense and time commitment of a lengthy dinner.

3. I always use nice plates and silverware. Even if it's take-out. Even if it's just me.

4. I take a lot of photos. And they're not simply posted on Facebook or stored away on my hard drive.

With my great publicist and friend Carissa Villacorta

My pictures rotate constantly on the wall of our living room on the big flat screen TV. These images of family and friends are a simple reminder of all our blessings.

5. I always play music. One of my friends once told me that my life has a soundtrack. She was referring to the fact that I always had music playing in the background as I cooked, studied, got ready to go out, etc. Sometimes I sing along to the latest hits, other times I just have soft instrumental music playing as I focus on work. Nowadays it's often classical music from *Baby Einstein!*

Lunching with some of my favorite Singapore ladies

The Perfect Blend

My super cool dad taking me for a spin in our family AMC
Ambassador station wagon

OPPOSITES ATTRACT

*W*HETHER CONSCIOUSLY OR NOT, one way my mother added color to her life was by marrying my father. "Two perfectly matched polar opposites" is how my brother and I described our parents on the invitation we had designed for their fortieth wedding anniversary. "Jose, a confident free spirit who takes pleasure in challenging authority. Lenore, a soft spoken, charming artist who appreciates order and harmony."

We even ordered personalized oil and vinegar bottles for the occasion with a label that read "The Perfect Blend." I feel fortunate to have been raised by this combination of parents. Sure, the same old arguments could grow tiresome. How many times would dad insist on testing border control while mom squirms in the passenger seat? But mostly it provided good balance and a whole lot of color. To this day, whenever they start their banter, my brother begins belting out the opening theme song to *All in the Family*, a 1970s sitcom, which featured gruff WWII veteran Archie Bunker, who often argued with everyone including his wife Edith. "Songs that made the hit parade ..." he uses an impeccable shrill old lady voice, which usually eases the tension.

My mother often recounts that one of the reasons she became interested in my father was *Lolo* Toni, my paternal grandfather. When my parents met, *Lolo* Toni had just retired from the Philippine Department of Foreign Affairs after nearly two decades of being abroad. What impressed my mother so much about *Lolo*

My community leader father performing the *tinikling*, a popular traditional Philippine dance, during a Philippine Independence Day celebration in Vancouver

Toni was not his Consul General title, his stories about various heads of state, or even his self-made success. It was his laid back and easygoing manner. My mother's father was quite the contrary. Justin and I grew up hearing stories about how tense my mother's household was with *Lolo* Seny as the head of it. Apparently all hell would break loose over something as minor as a misplaced pair of scissors. He was a very particular man, a strict father, and a stern employer. To say my mother and her three siblings walked on eggshells as they were growing up would be a huge understatement. Anything could set off their father whether it was their helper forgetting to put milk out with the coffee, one of the children asking permission to go out with friends, or someone bringing up an improper topic over dinner.

There was a broad range of "improper" as far as *Lolo* Seny was concerned. It wasn't just the usual uncouth matters you know not to discuss, such as a description of something you saw in a public restroom or the grotesque way a character was killed off in *The Walking Dead*. In the Raquel-Santos household, inappropriate topics included seemingly neutral subjects like dental appointments and funerals. To this day, my mother still hesitates to mention certain things at the dinner table.

"So when did you bump into *Tita* Fe?" I might ask.

"At the dentist—" my mother would cut herself short before glancing over apologetically at Alex. "Oh, I'm so sorry to talk about the dentist, you're still eating …"

"No worries," Alex will teasingly assure her between bites, "I can still keep this *adobo* down."

We're always amused by what topics fall under the scope of "improper."

"Just think of Downton," my mother will say. "Would they discuss it over dinner at *Downton Abbey*?" This was her litmus test.

And so I grew up with this image of my grandfather as a Spanish-Filipino Jack Nicholson meets Kevin Arnold's dad from *The Wonder Years*, which is why it was incredibly shocking for me years later to find a box full of the warmest letters he had written my mother when she and my father first immigrated to the US

Lolo Toni meeting Queen Beatrice of the Netherlands

Lolo Toni in his role as the elected Chairman of the United Nations Commission for Unification and Rehabilitation of Korea

Consul General Antonio Lim (*Lolo* Toni)

Attorney Arsenio Raquel-Santos
(*Lolo* Seny)

My father (center) with fellow "diplobrats"
at The American University in Cairo

With Prime Minister of Malaysia Tungku Abdul Rahman

One of many Philippine cultural evenings organized by my parents in Vancouver

and Canada. "My dearest Nore, I am so proud of what you have accomplished ..." or "Dearest Nore, I have always dreamed of having a granddaughter ..." My mother explained that *Lolo* Seny became much less tense as she and her siblings got older. Maybe everyday stresses just lessened so he could relax more, she once pondered. His four children went to the prestigious University of the Philippines, they all seemed to be happily married, and they were giving him grandchildren. Life was good.

Lolo Toni, on the other hand, appeared to be from an entirely different generation, if not planet. One of the first times my mother met him, she and my father (and a chaperone, of course) were stopping by the family home in Quezon City before going to a party. My mother couldn't help but pick up on the relaxed atmosphere as my father's five other siblings were coming in and out of the house while their father sat in the living room reading the paper.

My parents and fellow Filipino community leaders

It was dinnertime as my parents were leaving, so my mother asked, "What about your father? Who will prepare dinner for him?" It was the Philippines so there were always helpers in the kitchen who would whip up something but what she was really asking was, "Who's going to oversee the table setting and the food that goes out to your father?"

"He's fine," my father answered.

Lolo Toni smiled and assured her, "I'll take care of myself."

My mother was awestruck. This was highly unusual, not only compared to her father but to all Filipino fathers she knew. Maybe it was all his experience abroad or maybe he was just inherently easy going. Whatever the case, my mother remembers thinking at that moment, *If Didi is even half of what his father seems, this is a good man …* [3]

---

[3] "Didi" is my father's nickname.

Lolo Toni was from Santa Cruz, a small town in the island province of Marinduque, located in the middle of the Philippine Islands. His father was a Chinese baker and his mother a home-maker. He was one of five children and his family lived a simple life. After finishing high school in Marinduque, *Lolo* Toni was accepted into the University of the Philippines (UP), which was no easy task for a young man from the province since UP was the premier school across the country. Top students from elite high schools in Manila vied for limited spots but *Lolo* Toni passed the rigorous entrance exams and gained acceptance.

From there, he took up law and, despite the worldwide depression in the 1930s, secured job after job in both the private and public sectors, even starting his own practice. *Lolo* Toni began to make a name for himself as someone above politics when it came to the welfare of the country and its people. So much so that he was appointed to the Department of Foreign Affairs under then Vice-President and concurrent Secretary of Foreign Affairs Elpidio Quirino, who later became the sixth President of the Philippines. *Lolo* Toni rose through the ranks through assignments in Korea, Pakistan, Egypt, and Italy. Not too shabby for a small-town boy. To think, I just knew *Lolo* Toni as a distinguished-looking elderly Asian man who liked to take long walks and smoke a pipe.

When my parents met, *Lolo* Toni had just retired in the Philippines and the whole family had returned with him from Rome. My father and his siblings were what we have now come to call "third culture kids." The first culture refers to the culture of the country from which the parents originated, the second culture refers to the culture in which the family currently resides, and the third culture refers to the amalgamation of these two cultures. They had a lifetime of interesting stories from countries around the world. These were particularly fascinating to my mother, who had spent her whole life in Manila up to that point. Between my father's firsthand description of the Egyptian pyramids, his fascinating account of meeting the pope, and *Lolo* Toni's good nature, my mother inevitably put my father in the "high potential" box.

Of course, along with the captivating stories and charming persona came the flip side of the coin. My father and his siblings were diplomat kids and, well, let's just say they don't call them "diplobrats" for nothing. They were used to getting special treatment, had access to everything, and rules just didn't apply to them. To this day, when my father comes across a "Do Not Enter" sign, he sees a welcome mat. This drives my mother, the constant rule follower, just batty. "Don't worry," he likes to say teasingly, "my father's the mayor." (Interestingly, my father's grandfather *was* actually the mayor when his mother was growing up in Santa Cruz in the 1920s.)

I used to wonder why my father never seemed particularly impressed by fancy hotels and dinners the same way my mother was. Later on, I realized that it's simply a matter of "been there, done that." For my mother, it was the complete opposite. After all, she didn't get on a plane until her twenties. Heck, she barely got out of the house until her twenties. This is also one of the reasons they have very different ideas of the perfect vacation. My mother is content with a comfortable hotel and a good book. Enjoying nearby art museums and shopping is a bonus. My father's ideal vacation is the complete opposite. If left to him, we would barely set foot in the hotel. We would be out and about exploring the city (preferably one with a healthy amount of political unrest to keep things interesting) and winging everything including where to eat, where to hop on and off the bus, who to meet, and what to see.

Ever since my brother and I were old enough to have influence over (and funds for) family travel plans, we were always trying to think of suitable places to go with my polar opposite parents. Havana, Cuba, was one destination that Justin and I identified as a middle ground. The fact that Americans were banned from traveling there made it that much more intriguing for all of us. We weren't US citizens, or even permanent residents, so we drove to Toronto and went as Canadian tourists. There was something so cool about being able to tell your friends you were going to Cuba. "No big deal, we just want to go before Fidel

Castro passes away and Habana becomes another Miami," we would casually say, including the 'b' for good measure. It turned out to perfectly suit both my parents' needs.

Even the way my parents met is very fitting for their personalities. It was Holy Week in Santa Cruz, Marinduque, home to the annual Moriones festival. The "Moriones" are men and women in costumes and masks replicating the biblical Roman soldiers. My mother's aunt, *Tita* Rita, happened to be married to my father's uncle and they had invited my mother and her brother Francis to spend the holiday with them in the province.

Santa Cruz was where my father, his siblings, and their cousins typically spent every Holy Week. My mother remembers seeing all of them playing guitar and singing, drinking, and laughing. Educated all her life by the strict nuns from College of the Holy Spirit, she was brought up to believe Holy Week was supposed to be solemn. *Look at all these young kids*, she remembers thinking. In reality, my twenty-six-year-old mother was about the same age as everyone else but her formal ways always made her seem much older.

My father noticed my mother and remembers how prim and proper she was. *Challenge accepted!* He was intrigued by this conservative-looking young woman and wanted to find out what her deal was. He went up to her and *Tito* Francis and, to his surprise, it turned out to be a "pretty great" conversation and he invited them to a party that evening. My mother excused herself and went inside the house. When she returned, she told my father that her aunt approved and she and her brother would join.

My father was delighted, but it quickly dawned on him that he had to act fast to organize a party since, in typical fashion, he had been making it up. With the help of many cousins and friends, he was able to throw together a modest party at an ancestral home in Bundok[4]. As my father recalls, "The evening went very well in

---

[4] The American expression "boondocks" actually stems from the Tagalog word bundok. It originally referred to a remote rural area but now it is often applied to any out-of-the-way city or town.

terms of getting to know your mom. I am pretty sure we didn't speak to anyone except each other the whole night. We covered so many subjects from work, travel, relationships, future plans, hopes, and dreams that before the night ended, I found myself inviting her once again to another non-existing party the following day. I wanted the conversation to continue and never end."

The following day, however, was Good Friday, a very holy day in Santa Cruz. Tradition required there to be fasting the whole day, no music, and no unnecessary conversation among friends or even among family. As the nuns explained, "This day is to be dedicated in re-living the passion of Christ through personal sacrifices and abstentions." In other words, not the optimal circumstances for my father's made-up party.

Since nothing is a problem for my father, he simply proposed to his cousins and friends that they host their party up in the mountains away from the town people. Sure, there was no electricity or running water but somehow he convinced everyone to trek up with food, drinks, kerosene lamps, and a portable record player. It was all worth it, he recalls, especially since walking up the mountains in the dark was the perfect excuse to hold my mother's hand.

A rare informal photo of my mother's family in the late 1940s

My parents' recent 40th wedding anniversary at the Official Residence
of the Philippine Permanent Representative to the UN

With Permanent Representative to the UN Libran Cabactulan and Mrs. Fe Cabactulan

My father and fellow international students

My grandmother, *Lola* Ely, with my mother, siblings and friends in the 1950s

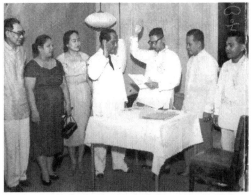

My grandfather taking his oath from Vice President Carlos P. Garcia who would later become President of the Philippines

My father, his future brother-in-law Riadh and his younger brother Eduardo

My father and his sister Nori playing guitar for their mother

My mother in her late twenties

One of my favorite photos of my mother

18th birthday

Celebrating 40 years with laughter and love

My parents after Sunday brunch on the Lower East Side
of Manhattan

HELLO FROM NARITA
(AND OTHER CONTRADICTIONS)

Leading By [Not Necessarily Good] Example

IN MANY WAYS, my father is one big contradiction. For starters, he has this masterful way of not leading by example. He broke every rule and expected us never to do so. He pushed harder than my mother for us to get high grades; meanwhile, we knew he had been a mediocre if not poor (or let's just say easygoing) student. He had no rules growing up but he raised us as strict as could be. I'm not sure how he did it but his double standard worked.

He continues this approach with his grandchildren. "A toothbrush is very personal. You must only use your own," my father explained in the voice of Confucius to Carlos after he caught him using his sister Isabel's *Frozen* toothbrush. I couldn't keep a straight face as he lectured my son on the importance of personal hygiene when all I could think about was my mother's horrified

My father and my husband

expression whenever we were on a trip and she saw my father using her toothbrush because he'd forgotten his own.[5]

No matter how many times my mother would frantically exclaim, "How can you expect them to do this when you do that?" my father's response was always calm and consistent: "I'm showing them what *not* to do."

---

[5] My mother was appalled when she read this section and wanted me to change "toothbrush" to "comb." I told her it wouldn't have the same effect.

Sappy Times

My father doesn't express feelings out loud but he is the biggest sap when it comes to writing. I first noticed this when I came across old birthday cards he had written my mother (some of these were memorialized in our photo albums). I began experiencing it myself firsthand when my parents started traveling on their own to the Philippines when we got older. My mother's cousin, *Tita* Chris, worked at Japan Air Lines so they would often use JAL to fly to Manila, stopping over in Tokyo. The layover on this flight was a long one, sometimes up to eight hours. My parents would look for an Internet station at the airport (this was way before ubiquitous Wi-Fi) so they could log onto AOL and let us know they had almost reached their destination. My father's subject line was always, "Hello from Narita." From there, he would proceed to tell us how much he loved and missed us and how we meant the world to him. I don't know if he was thinking "just in case there's an accident" or if he's like me and airplanes simply make him contemplative and nostalgic. Whatever the case, I loved these emails

An old letter written by my father (who never expresses such sentiment aloud)

and always said that if I ever wrote a book about my dad, I would call it, "Hello from Narita." He'll have to settle for a sub chapter.

The only time Justin and I have ever seen my father cry is when we were at the movie theater watching *Mrs. Doubtfire*, a comedy film starring the late Robin Williams who plays a divorced father pretending to be a nanny in order to have more access to his children. I was concentrating on quietly pulling out the candy stash I had snuck in from the Duane Reade drugstore across the street when Justin turned over to me and said, "I think Dad's crying!" I looked over and, sure enough, my father was tearing up as Robin Williams was giving a speech about how he didn't want to lose custody of his children because they meant so much to him. When we asked him about it later he admitted he got choked up because he couldn't imagine not being able to see his kids. It was a heartfelt answer that we weren't expecting since our father never said these things out loud. "Who wants a Junior Mint?" was my response, but this always left a lasting impression on Justin and me.

Crazy Asian Man

While my father rarely ever gets worked up or angry, he can turn on "Crazy Asian Man" like it's nobody's business. With him, frustrating customer service calls have gone something like this:

After a half hour on hold or between transfers, my father raises his voice and angrily says, "Listen, I've explained this three times already and each time I'm passed off to someone else. Either directly address my concern now or close my account!"

"Okay, sir, but first I need to authenticate you again. What is your password?"

My father heaves a sigh before saying, "Happy," in a most serious tone.

"Sir, that's not working. Is there another password it might be?"

Another exasperated sigh, "Smile." These were really our family passwords.

"Sorry, sir. That still doesn't work."

"Well then, try 'smiles' with an 's,'" my father sounds impatient but the bright and bubbly family passwords make the grumpy customer act lose effect, causing the customer service rep to hold back giggles.

My mother, however, always makes a point to be polite and cheerful with phone reps, particularly telemarketers. We usually screen our calls and have the answering machine pick up, but if we're on the phone when call waiting comes through, then we're out of luck. Even when trying to ignore the call waiting, there are intermittent pauses on the line that are equally distracting.

"Just one moment, I have a call waiting," my mother would say.

"Hello ...? Yes, it is ... Hi, how are you? Sure, but I do have someone else on the other line ... Great! Maybe you can call back ..." Many people simply hang up the line when they realize it's a telemarketer but my mother is always kind and pleasant. She says it's because she knows it's someone's child on the other end of the phone. "I always think, what if you or Justin were doing this job? How would I hope people were speaking to you?" Another litmus test.

This was a considerate practice, which my father generally incorporated as well. It's a good thing too because the fact of the matter is you never know who is on the other end of the phone. When I was doing the global management program at Citi, Ajay Banga was the executive sponsor. At the time, Ajay was the Co-CEO of Citi's Global Consumer Bank. He was a huge advocate of management programs influenced by the fact that he began his career as a management trainee at Nestlé India. As he often explains, here he learned the value of working across a variety of businesses and functions.

Ajay is one of those individuals who just exude leadership. He also has the ability to make you feel like you're the most important person in the room, a quality attributed to a number of public figures and especially former President Bill Clinton. I had the opportunity to meet President Clinton when I was fundraising for Hillary's campaign in 2008. He had just stepped off the stage when we were introduced.

"And where is it you work?" he asked as John Legend sang in the background.

"I'm at Citibank," I said loudly as I tiptoed. He was even taller than I imagined.

"Ah! So you must know Mr. Banga! He has got to be one of the most charismatic people I have ever met ..." he told me. *Wow,* I remember thinking. When Bill Clinton says that about someone, you better believe that person must be able to charm the pants off anybody.

The interview process for the new global management program was pretty intense. Donald Trump's reality show *The Apprentice* had just come out and those of us who went through the internal process described it as something similar—minus the drama, bad comb-over, and cliché "You're fired." We were shuffled from one interviewer to another, given a case study and evaluated

A quick photo I snapped seconds before meeting him

real time by a panel sitting in front of us as we worked through the solution, put in a holding room to wait while the judges deliberated. Those who made it were sent to meet with then CEO of Citi Cards, Steve Freiberg, before jumping on the subway to midtown to meet with Ajay, then CEO of Citibank North America.

Ironically, the most calming part of the stressful process was the high-pressure interview with Ajay, which took place in his office on the executive floor of the Citi headquarters at 399 Park Avenue. By this time, I had only been on that floor on two occasions. The first time was a Women & Company meeting with Lisa Caputo, Former Press Secretary to First Lady Hillary Clinton. The second time was when I went to meet a mentor for coffee and I bumped right into then CEO Sandy Weill and Reverend Jesse Jackson. It was intimidating just to step off the elevator onto that floor.

Ajay had this way of connecting with everyone, including me. Sure, we talked about the management program, why he wanted to start it, why I wanted to do it. But he seemed to be more interested in who I was as a person. What inspired and motivated me. My values. It didn't take more than a few minutes for this conversation to be about my family. My parents. Their journey.

So, it shouldn't have been a complete surprise one year later when Ajay was doing my performance review (yes, he insisted on personally doing our reviews) and he said, "You've done extremely well. You should take your parents out to dinner tonight. And you should tell them that we're very lucky to have you. Actually, *I* should tell them that we're very lucky to have you ... What's their telephone number?"

Shortly after that conversation, I had to get to another meeting. When I returned to my desk, my father called, saying, "So I got a call from an Ajay Banga ... He said, 'This is Ajay Banga calling from Citibank' and I thought it was a telemarketer. It's a good thing your mother reminds us to be friendly no matter who is on the phone." Ajay is now the President and CEO of MasterCard. Last year one of my colleagues asked if I could introduce him to Ajay over email. I had only exchanged a few messages with Ajay since he left the bank in 2009 but I was comfortable making this introduction. It took not even five minutes for Ajay to reply back to my email and ask, "How are your parents?"

Not Your Average Señorito

No one has more Filipino pride than my father yet, in many ways, he has very few traits of Filipino men (at least, Filipino men from his generation). I guess that's not surprising considering how progressive his father was.

Sometimes it's the reactions of my friends that remind me how independent my father is compared to his contemporaries. A couple of years ago, he came with Alex and me to Macao to watch a Manny Pacquiao fight. Like many Filipino men, my father has been following Pacquiao ever since he was fighting in the flyweight division (he has since become the first and only eight-division world champion). Alex quickly became a fan and soon we all found ourselves flying out for his fights. Typically they were in Las Vegas and tickets were in the hundreds of dollars range if you were lucky. But even if you didn't go to the actual fight, being around the high energy was worth it plus you could attend the live weigh in, which was free and open to the general public.

The Macao fight was scheduled on a Sunday morning so the night before everyone who was in town for it convened around McSorley's Ale House, the Irish bar at The Venetian. One of the great things about fight weekend in Macao is that celebrity sightings are pretty much narrowed down to one corner of The Venetian. If you hung out around there all weekend, you were almost guaranteed to see David Beckham, Billy Baldwin, and APL from Black Eyed Peas in addition to Manny Pacquaio and his entourage.

We were out with a number of Filipino friends, some from Vancouver, some from New York, and some from Singapore. Fans were flying in from all around the world to support Manny

With APL from Black Eyed Peas at Manny Pacquio's first fight in Macau

Pacquiao. At one point in the evening, my father told me he was going off to find a restroom.

"Hey, where's your dad?" my friend Derrick asked. Derrick grew up in Manila but he and his wife, Ria, were now living in Singapore. We had met through our mutual friend, Christine, and shortly afterward Ria and I discovered we were cousins. This wasn't unusual in the small global Filipino community.

"He just went to the bathroom," I told Derrick over someone's live rendition of Billy Joel's "Pianoman."

Derrick looked surprised. "But you and Alex are still here …" I didn't understand where he was going with this until he followed up and asked, "Do you want me to go accompany him?"

Ah, now I got it. "No, no, he's fine," I smiled. It was such a kind gesture of him to ask, but picturing Derrick accompanying my father to the restroom was an amusing thought.

My father and Alex with sportswriter Ryan Songalia (second from left) and our good friend Derrick Santos (second from right)

Psyched for the fight

Making opening remarks at a victory celebration after Corazon Aquino became President of the Philippines in 1986

My father and I with the Rebodos sisters who were some of my closest childhood friends

Hands-on *Lolo*

Many Filipino men from my father's generation are accustomed to others doing things for them. "He's such a *señorito*," was a common descriptor. Historically, this was used to describe a young man from a landed Spanish family who had people waiting on him hand and foot.

My father doesn't fall into that particular category so sometimes I would hear people comment, "He's not very Filipino."

In many ways, that's not true. He is better versed on Filipino news, politics, and pop culture than most. He watches TFC (The Filipino Channel) any chance he gets. He can tell you about the latest congressional hearings in Manila, he knows all the latest plots of *Be Careful With My Heart*, and the GMA network variety shows play in the background of my parents' apartment all day on Sunday.

Of course, I understand why he doesn't come across as a typical Filipino. I grew up with my father leading demonstrations against the Marcos regime, driving across the continent to pick up visiting relatives, and doing loads of laundry and other household chores. He drove my mother to and from the art studio every evening, helped my brother and me with our homework, and made the best chicken curry. There wasn't a term for it back then, but today he would be the poster person for the #heforshe movement.

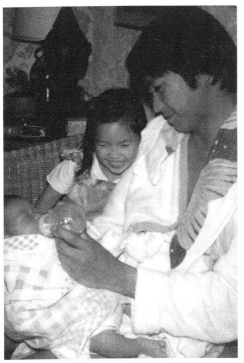

Hands-on father

New immigrants to Canada

ONE LEG AT A TIME

*W*HILE MY FATHER'S CONSTANT RULE BREAK-
ING AND ENVELOPE pushing has given my mother more
than a healthy level of stress, even she has to admit that the family has benefitted from his unabashed approach on at least a few
critical occasions, most notable being their immigration interview
for Canada.

One of the biggest lessons I've learned from my father is
never be intimidated by anyone. "He still puts his pants on one leg
at a time," my father will say. When I was twelve and going to my
first New Kids on the Block concert, he heard me shrieking about
the idea of seeing Jordan Knight in person. "No need to get so excited, the guy still puts his pants on one leg at a time." Years later,
I remember telling him that I was anxious about meeting former
President Jimmy Carter on a Habitat for Humanity project. Again,
"Don't be nervous, he still puts his pants on one leg at a time."

This non-intimidation quality of my father's has served
him well. My parents would have never made it into Canada without it. Anyone who has crossed a border knows how standoff-
ish immigration officers can be. You can have all the documents

required, you can have every reason to be there, and you may even be a citizen. It can still be a nerve-wracking event. Much more so when you're on the brink of overstaying your visa and trying to gain entry to a new country. This was the case for my parents after they had been waiting three months for their immigration interview.

"I'm sorry, we're going to have to decline," the immigration officer said, closing the file. My mother stood up to leave.

"Can I ask why we're not being approved?" my father wasn't going anywhere.

"Unfortunately, I can't approve your application because you don't have enough work experience," the immigration officer explained before standing up to end the conversation.

"But that's a good thing!" My father put on his positive spin. The immigration officer looked very confused and vaguely intrigued. My father continued, "No experience also means no negative experience. Companies can mold me from scratch. They can train me from the bottom up."

"This is true," the officer conceded, "but it's just a tough job market right now. You'll be hard pressed to find someone who will even open the door."

"Then I'll knock on another door," my father argued with conviction. "And if that doesn't work, I'll try another. And another. Eventually I will find a company that will be thrilled to have someone like me."

The immigration officer realized my father would not let up on this one and he needed another reason to decline. "I believe that may very well be true but the fact of the matter is that we're just not accepting many applicants to Vancouver at this time," he stood up again.

My father stayed seated. "Well, how about Montreal?"

The immigration officer sat down again and opened the file. "It doesn't say anywhere here you speak French," he commented as he closed it and attempted to stand once more. My mother followed.

"*Oui, oui! Je parle français!*" my father confidently said one of the five French phrases he knew.

The immigration officer cracked a smile, "I appreciate the effort but I don't think so. I'm sorry but I have to take the next interview."

My mother stood for the third time as the officer did, and my father gestured for her to sit down again. "Officer, Montreal was really our first choice but we have friends in Vancouver who have been convincing us to join them. But if there are no more spaces for Vancouver, we would like to be considered for Montreal. With my skills and my persistence, I'll be able to get a job there," my father was convincing.

The immigration officer sighed, "Okay, let me see if I can get one of the French speaking colleagues to interview you." He started dialing a number on his phone. My mother was horrified since she knew my father's French capabilities or lack thereof. My father remained cool as a cucumber.

"He's not there, let me try someone else," the immigration officer was now dialing a series of numbers.

Then there was a knock at the door. "Excuse me, Officer. I need to send in the next interview," said one of the assistants, peeking in.

"Alright, alright," he responded. "I can't reach anyone and I really have to move this along." He stamped the documents and the rest is history.

My father always says that more often than not you have a fifty-fifty shot. His philosophy is that if one person is determining your fate, you have to give it everything you've got.

It's funny, but for as much as my mother talks about my father's confidence, they both have a healthy level of self-esteem if you ask me. I mean this in the best possible way. My mother may have been a shy Catholic schoolgirl but those nuns from College of the Holy Spirit must have known how to instill self-worth. While she was quiet and non-threatening, my mother was never insecure. Criticism rolled off her back and lit a fire within.

One of many family road trips

Several years back, I was dating someone who came from a very successful family. On one occasion, his parents invited my family over for dinner. I was excited about the idea of our parents bonding and chatting away. Unfortunately, from the moment we stepped into their home until the second we left, my boyfriend's father was on the phone. My boyfriend's mother, on the other hand, graciously greeted us and kept us entertained while drinks were served in the sitting room. A few times she excused herself to go upstairs and check on her husband but he never followed her back down. We continued to hear his muffled voice on the phone until finally Boyfriend's mother said, "Why don't we just start dinner then?"

To be honest, I didn't think too much of it at the time. I knew Boyfriend's father was a very busy man so I didn't take it personally. But my mother did.

"He just had a lot of business going on, Mom. They're working on this deal ..." I defended Boyfriend's father on the drive home.

"If it were the Queen downstairs, he would have found a way to step out and greet her properly," my mother replied. I think it was the immigrant experience in Commonwealth Canada that makes "the Queen" a common reference in our family.

"Okay, fine," I chuckled with resignation. "He probably would have come down to say hello to the Queen ..."

"You are more important than the Queen," she said defiantly. Justin was now roaring with laughter but my mother explained, "You are the person his son wants to marry. If you're a father, what could be more important than meeting the family of the person your son wants to marry?"

No one could argue with that.

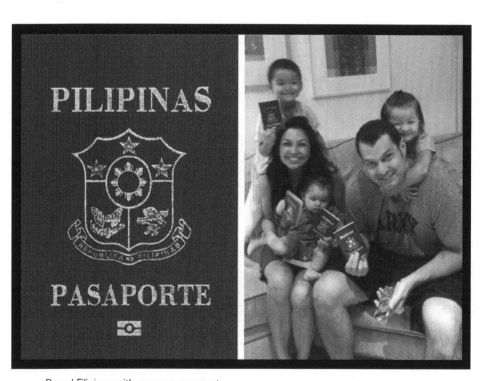

Proud Filipinos with our new passports

Positively Filipino

It's All Good

ANYONE WHO HAS READ *Don't Forget the Soap* knows all about my mother's faith-based positivity. It all happens for a reason as far as she's concerned, and there's always a silver lining.

My father has a similar brand of optimism. In all my years, I have never heard my father complain. One of his favorite sayings is, "It's only a problem if you make it a problem." Instead of thinking, "We *have* to wait in line," my father says, "We *get* to wait in line." He'll continue, "This means we have time to rest for a moment. We can talk to each other and reflect." One time we found a loaf of bread squashed at the bottom of a grocery bag and my father's first response was, "That's a nice reason to go to the park and feed the ducks."

Sometimes Justin and I even try to get a complaint out of my father. There are many times when I've seen my father exhibit patience but none more often as standing in the car. Standing in the car is a common practice when you live in New York City.

Parking is tough, especially on weekdays before 7:00 p.m. or on Saturdays between 11:00 a.m. and 5:00 p.m. or, who are we kidding, parking is a bear any day of the week with the exception of Sunday. So, often someone just waits or "stands" (the official parking term) in the car while the other family members go about their business. My father would "stand" in the car while my mother and I did our shopping at Macy's. I would "stand" in the car while my father was showing an apartment. My father, Justin, and I would often "stand" in the car while waiting for my mother to finish from the art studio.

In retrospect, it's hard to think that we would be able to do all this "standing" without smartphones. The most entertainment we would have is 106.7 LITE FM playing the hits of the 1960s, 1970s, 1980s, and today.

"Dad, do you ever get tired of waiting in the car?" I asked one day as "How Deep Is Your Love" by the Bee Gees faded into a commercial.

He just smiled and kept tapping his fingers on the steering wheel. "When else would we get to practice our harmonies?"

The other week, while on a family vacation in Thailand, Justin and I were with my father and we all ordered ice cream. Justin got his staple mint chocolate chip, I got my classic chocolate and pistachio combo, and my father uncharacteristically ordered rum raisin. He was typically a vanilla or strawberry guy. "Why'd you go for that?" I asked.

"There was vanilla and strawberry in our banana split yesterday. I thought I'd try something different."

When the ice cream came, we all went about trying each other's as we usually did.

"Oh, that's a great mint chocolate chip. I love when they throw some Oreo cookie in there!" I said to Justin.

"Yours is really good too. The chocolate almost tastes like Nutella," Justin observed. He then went in to try Dad's rum raisin. "Whoa! That's terrible," Justin winced.

"Lots of people would love this," my father smiled as he defended his ice cream.

I went to try for myself. It was pretty bad. I'm not a big rum raisin person but I can appreciate the flavor when Alex or his mother (both rum raisin fans) orders it. This one was way too strong.

"Come on, Dad. Just call it what it is," Justin teased. He would often try to get my father to break his positive spin.

"If you like rum, you'd really like this," my father was sticking to his guns.

"But would you order it again?" Justin wouldn't relent.

"It might not be my first choice," my father conceded a little bit.

"What about your eightieth choice?" Justin persisted, "Would it be your eightieth choice?" He wanted the full admission.

Strolling around Columbia University on a recent trip back to New York

Making the Most of Everything

Not only do my parents make the best of everything, they also make the most of everything.

For my mother, it's all about reusing and recycling. For instance, while she was teaching at UNIS, she would have three or four bulletin boards around her classroom. They would say things like, "Spring is here," "What is the weather today?" and "My Family." Like all teachers, she would change the boards every month or so. Unlike all the other teachers, she would carefully take down each individual item from her classroom boards. Most of her colleagues would crumple the whole board display in one big swoop before squeezing it into the trash. My mother would have her students take down each letter, each cloud, and each raindrop, remove the scotch tape from behind them, and put them individually in Ziploc bags. She would then send them to School of Love and Hope, her aunt's school for disabled children in the Philippines.

Today, she is teaching my children how to do the same. Carlos and Isabel save macaroni and cheese boxes to make cardboard robots (toilet paper rolls are turned into arms and legs, and raisin containers into feet), packing Styrofoam is used for canvases, and scraps of wrapping paper transformed into Christmas cards.

My father has his own way of making the most of everything, which often makes for amusing anecdotes like the ones that follow.

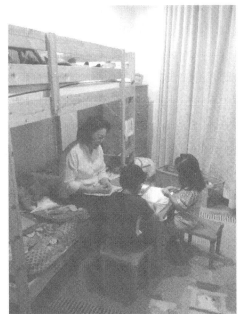

My mother's regular
arts and crafts sessions
with the kids

Tissue box faces

Our first visit to New York City back in 1983. You could never rain on our parade...

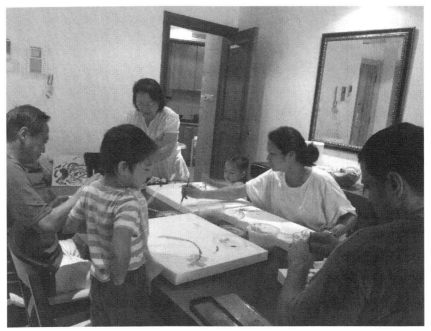

My mother's idea to use the styrofoam from a care package as painting canvases

With ever supportive *Lolo*

Happy Valentine's Day

More arts and crafts with *Lola*

While their toys were being shipped to Hong Kong, my mother helped the kids create toys of their own

The styrofoam artworks are now hanging in the children's bathroom

Enjoying our "timeshare" in Phuket

DIRTY LAUNDRY

*W*HEN WE FIRST MOVED TO ASIA, Alex's boss gave us a complimentary stay at his Marriott Vacation Club. You know, one of those free visits for four days and three nights where the only catch is that you need to meet with an "Owner Referral Executive." The Marriott Vacation Club is essentially a timeshare but we never call it that. "Timeshare" is a term of the 1980s that got stashed away with Sharper Image and Radio Shack. And my beloved Cabbage Patch Kids.

Timeshares didn't always have a negative stigma. When we were growing up we would associate timeshare with our "rich" *Titos* and *Titas*. *Tito* Armand's family owned a timeshare, as did *Tito* Benny and *Tita* Nanette, and *Tito* Romy and *Tita* Belinda. When *Tito* Armand's family was moving back to the Philippines, my mother took over their timeshare. For one of Justin's birthdays, I saw her put a certificate of sorts into an envelope.

"What's that?" I asked.

"Something very special," she told me as she showed me the certificate. "It has always been one of my dreams to own a piece of a timeshare."

Really? I wondered. I never quite understood the appeal of timeshares. It seemed like it was just one specific week of the year to go to one specific place. Maybe I was missing something. Then, I realized that for my mother, a timeshare meant she had made it. We all have things like that. For Alex, it's a kitchen island. He has always wanted one of those big open kitchens with a sleek kitchen island in the middle of it. I'm pretty sure he could have had one if we lived somewhere else but between the exorbitant rents of Manhattan, Singapore, and Hong Kong, it may still be a while.

Alex and I have been to a few timeshare presentations in our day and the Marriott one was relatively no pressure. Nothing like the insanity we experienced in Cabo San Lucas where the sales people had infiltrated into society. We would get in a taxi from the airport and even the driver would turn out to be an undercover timeshare person ("So, I bring you to Hilton after we stop by and see my friend …").

One night we went out to dinner and started chitchatting with the waiter. "So, how are you guys liking Cabo?" he asked as he poured our wine.

"It's great! The beach is beautiful and there's so much to do," we responded, keeping it general.

"Yeah, it's just too bad there are so many timeshare people bothering you though, right?" he smiled knowingly. We loved this guy!

"Yes! What is up with that?" We were now leaning in toward him, completely engaged.

"It's crazy," he started to say. "Some of these guys even pretend to be taxi drivers at the airport …"

"Yes, that happened to us!" We chimed in. He completely understood our situation.

"No!" He put on a great expression of disbelief. "Oh man, I'm so sorry you guys had to experience that …" We chatted for a good ten minutes. "So listen, before you guys leave, I'm just going to introduce you to my friend. He is nothing like those other timeshare people …"

Alex and I exchanged horrified glances. We had been had again!

Nevertheless, when we joined the Marriott Vacation Club in Phuket, my mother was impressed. "This kind of time-share wasn't even in my dreams," she commented the first time we stayed at the JW Marriott. It was a great set up. A roomy two bedroom villa with a full kitchen, a big round dining table with six comfortable chairs (this meant it would seat about a dozen Filipinos), a jacuzzi, a balcony overlooking the landscaped pool, and more. My father's favorite villa feature, however, was the en suite washer dryer.

As we were packing for our most recent Phuket trip, my father was going around the apartment from room to room asking, "Where are your dirty clothes?"

"In the back room," I heard Justin answer as he was putting a filter on his Instagram photo.

He moved to Carlos' room. "Hey Carlos, where do you put your dirty clothes?" He then entered my room. "How about you, Claire?"

Another one of Justin's famous Instagram posts when he joined us in Phuket

"In the hamper in my closet," I responded. "Why?"

"I'll pack them," he answered.

"What? Why?" Justin came into my room, equally curious.

"There's a washer and dryer in our place there, right? You know how much the dryer adds to your electricity bill?" he exclaimed.

"Dad, you don't need to pack dirty laundry for Phuket," I laughed.

"Savings, man," was all he said as he continued on his mission.

My father often throws in the word "man" when he's teaching us a lesson but still being lighthearted, though I think this only began when we were adults. "You have to learn some patience, man," he'll tell Justin, who might be complaining about having to wait in the car while my father has to drop off some paperwork.

We're not a big "games" family but we are always drawn to this
shuffleboard at the Turtle Village bar in Mai Khao Beach

At the Marriott Mai Khao Beach Club

Filipino MacGyver

"Resourceful and possessed of an encyclopedic knowledge of the physical sciences, he solves complex problems by making things out of stuff, along with his ever-present Swiss Army Knife. He prefers non-violent resolutions and prefers not to handle a gun." – From the "MacGyver" Wikipedia page.

Aside from the encyclopedic knowledge of the physical sciences (which my father could easily fake, by the way), this Wikipedia description of secret agent Angus MacGyver from the American action-adventure TV series could just as well be my dad.

The other day, Alex put bags of groceries down on the floor and a bottle of wine broke in one of the bags. He was about to throw it out when my father swooped in, took out all the broken glass, and turned the plastic bag into a wine carafe that we used for the remainder of the evening.

Another time, my father and I were wheeling groceries back from Great World City, the shopping center a couple blocks away from our home in Singapore. As he pulled the heavy load up the curb, the cart handle broke.

"Oh well, I guess we can throw this out," I said. I knew we could get another from the grocery for about $20 plus we had a spare—a Bounty cart we had received as a free gift after buying six rolls of paper towels.

"No, no. This can be fixed. I just need some glue," my father replied.

The following weekend we were back at Great World City with the Bounty cart. This time, as we were walking back to our condo, one of the wheels came loose and broke. "Okay, this one I can throw out. It's useless without a wheel," I pointed out.

"No, no. Now I can take the handle off that cart and put it on the other one. I just need to unscrew it and it will be as good as new." He went to grab his toolbox.

His fixes are not always sleek, they often involve crazy glue and duct tape, but they do the trick.

"There he goes gluing things again ..." my mother says. Crazy glue and duct tape often came between my mother and, say, a new car, so I understood the underlying resentment.

One time, we were driving along FDR Drive on our way to "stand" between 5th and 6th Avenues while we waited for my mother to finish a meeting at the Philippine Consulate.

"Hey, Dad," I said, noticing a piece of black electric tape covering the dashboard. "What's that?"

"I had to cover a light that kept blinking," he responded.

"What kind of light?" I didn't know much about cars but I knew the information on the dashboard was usually important.

"Something about maintenance required," he answered my question.

I laughed, and then said, "Well, then, don't you think it requires maintenance?"

"Nah, that's just something they do so the dealership can continue to make money," he said matter-of-factly. My father will only bring the car in to be checked if absolutely necessary.

"Hey, Dad," I started again, "your gas meter is always on empty. Shouldn't you get that fixed?"

"No need," he would say.

"Isn't it kind of important so you know when you need to get gas?"

"Nah, I can look at the mileage for that."

Value for Money

It's hard for my father to enjoy a massage and only recently have I realized why.

"How was the massage?" I asked.

"It was a little strong," he winced slightly.

"Well, then, why didn't you ask for lighter pressure when she asked?"

"I wanted to get the most value for my money." He proceeded to explain that you're actually paying for the massage therapist's amount of effort.

My father loves talking about value for money. I remember the time he wanted to take me to a new midtown Korean deli that had an extensive salad bar. In the 1990s, salad bars in New York City had taken on a whole new meaning. They had a variety of salads, cold food, and a hot food buffet bar. Pastas, barbecued chicken, sushi, mashed potatoes, and hummus all now qualified as "salad." The best part for my father was that it was pay-per-pound.

When we got to the cash register, the Korean lady weighed my father's plastic container. "One pound, $2.95."

My father looked proud of himself, as if he had just found the cure for cancer. "See that? I have fish, olives, artichokes, nuts, feta cheese ... All gourmet foods for less than three bucks!"

The Korean lady took my container and said, "Three pounds, $8.85."

"Whaaat?" My father exclaimed. He looked more closely at my plate. "Lasagna? Hard-boiled eggs? Cantaloupe? Are you kidding me? You have to have a strategy, man ..."

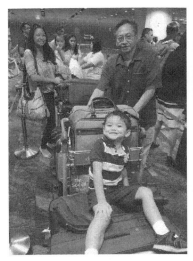

Family travels

Showing off our new fanny packs on a road trip to Washington DC in 1983

More Memories Than Our

Hearts Can Hold

Smart Parenting magazine feature and the Evernote mention

*T*HERE ARE TWO THINGS MY FRIENDS always say about me. The first is that I'm happy and the second is that I have a great memory. I'm convinced the two are related. Part of being happy is living in the moment and remembering the little things. Recently I've come to appreciate how memories play a big role in our family and how happy thoughts are integral to staying positive.

While I was living in Brazil, my parents and Justin came to visit for Christmas. I spent the first week showing them around Sao Paulo before driving to Rio to ring in the New Year. One perfect evening, we were enjoying a delicious *churrascaria* dinner on the sidewalk streets of Leblon, a beautiful neighborhood tucked away next to the famous Ipanema.

We were taking in the cosmopolitan charm and scenery when my mother remarked, "This is too much. We have more memories than our hearts can hold."

Justin, my father, and I looked at each other and then back at my mother. "Wow, Mom. Did you just come up with that?" We were thoroughly impressed. My mother did many things well but coming up with off-the-cuff one-liners was not typically one of them.

"Yes ... I don't know where it came from," she laughed.

"That was, like, really deep and profound," I couldn't help but exclaim.

"It must have been the Holy Spirit," she concluded. Now *that* sounded like our mother.

"More memories than our hearts can hold" became institutionalized in our book of family sayings like "Don't Forget the Soap" or "Who's going to tell you ... Nadeen?" (Yes, you'll have to read the first book.)

A few years later, when Apple started to re-emerge and re-dominate electronics, Justin and I decided to buy my mother an iPod for her birthday. "They're calling it 'the Walkman of the twenty-first century,'" Justin explained. "And you know what's really cool? We can engrave it on the back."

Now, I don't know who originally came up with the idea to engrave it with our latest family expression. I'd like to think it was me, but over the years my brother and I have become even more particular about who gets credit for ideas. It started over thirty years ago. I had opened the refrigerator one day looking for a snack. I saw leftover spaghetti sauce in a bowl, so I took it out, peeled off the Saran Wrap, and used a Nabisco saltine cracker to scoop out some congealed Bolognese. A-MA-ZING. For an eight year old who had never cooked before I felt like I had invented sliced bread. As I was on my third or fourth saltine scoop, Justin walked into the kitchen and asked what I was doing. Being the generous sister that I am, I gave him my meat sauce cracker to try and, no surprise, he loved it. He dropped the He-Man toy he had been holding and ran out of the kitchen, saying, "Mom, Dad, try this!"

I heard my parents "ooh" and "ahh" as their four-year-old son showed off what might as well have been *boeuf bourguignon* as far as I was concerned.

"Wow, Justin! Did you make this yourself?"

"This is sooo good! Great work!"

I was listening to all of this from the kitchen and couldn't take it. "No! *I* made it! That was *my* recipe!" Even at the age of eight, I knew I was being unreasonable. What made matters worse is that everyone including Justin seemed to be amused by my over-reaction.

To this day, Justin will still tease, "Remember how I invented that delicious 'cracker bolognese?'" He'll say with this cheeky grin.

This still happens today. I did an interview with *Smart Parenting* magazine and they asked how I managed my time. I told them all about my new favorite app called Evernote, which my brother had recommended to me. I have become much more social media savvy since writing and promoting my book, but Justin has been my go-to person for all things current and cool particularly with music and technology. He'll post a song to my Facebook page and write, "Here's a new song you'll love, Claire. It has old school 1990s beats." Or he'll send me a WhatsApp message with a link to Dubsmash, saying, "This is what the kids are doing these days." He's thirty-four, so either he's super hip or I'm super old.

I felt compelled to mention all this during my *Smart Parenting* interview so, of course, when the article came out there was prominent mention of Evernote but no corresponding mention of my brother.

"So ... you just found Evernote on your own, did you?" He teased with attitude after seeing the magazine.

And so, as the story goes, it was both of us who jointly came up with the brilliant idea to engrave the iPod for my mother with, "More memories than our hearts can hold."

As my mother was unwrapping the gift, she looked over the moon when she realized it was a brand new iPod. "Oh my, this is too much!"

"And look what it says on the back, Mom!" Justin and I practically said in unison.

She took a moment to read the engraving. "Wow ... unbelievable!"

Yes, it sure is pretty special, I remember thinking.

We all laughed out loud when she continued, "So this is Apple's tagline too?"

Enjoy the little things,
for one day you will look back and
realize they were the

Big Things

THINGS THAT CROSS MY MIND
AT THE DENTIST

*"Enjoy the little things because one day you may realize
they were the big things."* — Kurt Vonnegut

"*T*HE LITTLE THINGS" cross my mind and add color to my life. The 1980s family sitcoms we would watch always used to have one episode every couple seasons where the main characters sat around the living room coffee table, taking a trip down memory lane. I used to think it was the coolest thing because you'd get up to eight storyline highlights in one episode. Now I realize that the lead writers must have just been on holiday. The premise of these shows could be that one of the kids was interviewing the family for a school project.

"So, Dad, have you always wanted to work in television?"

"Why, yes, I have, Jennifer. I can't imagine doing anything else."

"Wait a second, Dad," one of the other kids would chime in. "I remember the time when you had some other aspiration, ahem, singing ..."

The show would then flash back to a scene from an earlier episode when the dad got up the nerve to sing karaoke at a big family wedding. After the hilarious rendition of "My Way," the foggy lens takes us back to real time when the dad says, "Okay, okay, but that's nothing compared to the ballet performance Alex did when he was trying to win over Ellen ..."[6] It was like the show's Greatest Hits in a one-hour special.

I've got my own version of Greatest Hits featuring my family and friends, and many times these reruns play in my head while I'm at the dentist. More than any other place on earth, the dentist (well, the dentist and church to be completely honest) is when I am left to my own thought devices. It's not sitting on an airplane when I can watch a movie or fall asleep. It's not even in the waiting room of the dentist when I can flip through a magazine or scroll through my phone. No, it's lying there on the dentist chair with my mouth open and my hands locked by my side when my thoughts can really wander.

My family would pay frequent visits to the dentist. Not because we had particularly bad teeth or anything, but we just ended up with a really great dentist who was also a family friend. My mother met Dr. Ricafrente AKA *Tita* Angie when her son JP was in her first first-grade class at UNIS in 1989. Dr. Ricafrente had migrated from the Philippines to the US several years back to start her own practice. Her office is located on the ground floor of a fancy residential building in Central Park South right in between The Plaza and Columbus Circle. Just purchasing that space in the early 1980s was a winning business strategy. Dr. Ricafrente met her husband John in New York City and they had JP two years later. With all they had in common, my mother and Dr. Ricafrente became fast friends and have remained close ever since.

My brother and I always describe Dr. Ricafrente as an "old school dentist." As second-generation Filipinos, we had heard

---

[6] Anyone familiar with 1980s sitcoms would know that this is a bad recreation of an old *Family Ties* episode.

plenty of stories about how dental hygiene worked back in the day in the Philippines. "They would tie one end of a string around your tooth and the other end on the doorknob of an open door. Then they would slam the door so hard your tooth could come out," I remember my father describing. To this day, I don't know whether there's truth to this or not. Dr. Ricafrente's methods were a far cry from such extremes but nevertheless the lady was thorough. Going for a cleaning with most dentists was pretty painless. A little polish here, a little rinse there. Dr. Ricafrente's cleaning, on the other hand, was quite intense. Your gums got a real workout, as she would go where no dental instrument had gone before. But when you left, boy, did you feel like you had a brand new set of teeth!

Of course, this is probably another reason my Greatest Hits played at the dentist. As soon as any discomfort set in, so did humorous vignettes of family and friends. Some favorite reruns that come to mind ...

Sleepovers and Rita Strikes

When my friends and I graduated from college and moved back to the city, I was the only one who had my own place. Some friends moved back in with their parents for a short period, others found roommates, and others moved in with their boyfriends. My studio on 46th Street between 2nd and 3rd became a clubhouse of sorts. I was fortunate that my parents encouraged me to save my summer income for a down payment for this apartment. It was 400 square feet of on-my-ownhood.

Every summer in college, I had managed to secure a summer internship at American Express (thanks to Yale Career Services and one very proactive alumnus). One of the many great things about this internship was that everything about it, including its salary, was designed for MBA students. Of course, there were adjustments made for the three of us who were still undergrads but, even so, it would be an understatement to say we were very lucky. I was in an even more enviable position because I didn't have to pay New York City rent during those summers since I was living at my parents' place in Waterside Plaza. I was beside myself the first time I saw my bi-weekly paycheck. Before I could go on my Club Monaco shopping spree, my parents were already doing real estate math for me.

It was a great call. Almost as soon as I left my college dorm I was able to move in to my New York City apartment. It took no time for my studio to feel like home. My father helped me paint the walls purple (like the *Friends* apartment) and pistachio green (this was admittedly influenced by my friend May's bedroom), we moved in the extra living room furniture (somehow my parents always have extra Filipino wood furniture lying around), we laid out two of the five Persian rugs we had acquired from my *Tita* Nori and *Tito* Riadh, and we set up the Sleepy's daybed (the same one we had bought our first year in New York back in 1988—Justin still uses this today, by the way). The 46th street studio was also home to my very first grown up piece of furniture, which was a mosaic table designed by the parents of one of my mother's former students. It's still one of my favorite belongings of all time. The mosaic tiles are violet and green (like my walls) and actual pieces of china were used to create a table setting design. The fact that Madonna and Antonio Banderas owned one of these was icing on the cake. And it sparked a good dinner conversation.

Back then, in my 400-square-foot studio, I hosted more than I do now in our 2,000-square-foot apartment. Six people could comfortably fit around my mosaic dining table and when I had more than six people over (this was more often than you might think) I went to my closet and pulled out our trusty folding *mahjong* table to expand the party. Justin would often joke that my closet was so stuffed he wouldn't be surprised if there was a little old lady living in it. I don't know why I thought that was so funny but the imagery still cracks me up today.

In addition to regular dinners, I hosted regular sleepovers. Coming back to New York City was a reunion for my closest high school friends and me. My doorman knew my high school friends May and Alexis by name and they never needed to get buzzed up.

May and Kristen on the night of "Rita Strikes"

At the time, May was working at then up and coming Foley and Corinna in the then up and coming Lower East Side, Alexis was taking acting classes at Lee Strasberg, and I was working in the financial district at American Express. We had a weekly ritual of meeting at my place in the evening, cooking up fish and couscous (Alexis was influencing our healthy diet), and hanging out until we fell asleep. It was during one of these sleepovers that Zomashi was born. Between our love of fashion and our love of spending time together, the three of us came up with the idea of starting a bold new fashion line. Alexis' middle name was Zoe, "ma" came from the Marie in my name, and May's last name, Oishi, inspired the last syllable. It was pure genius. We designed a flyer to look for a seamstress, we started talking to potential investors such as our most successful friends (David Rappa, Rafay Farooqui, and Sheldon Gilbert), and I even purchased the zomashi.com domain name. Nothing has officially transpired yet with Zomashi but I just checked and the domain name is still available, so you never know.

In September 2005, I was on a five-week project in New York in between assignments in Miami and Sao Paolo. My apartment was being rented out at the time, so Citi provided me with temporary housing for two months. It was a large studio down the street from Carnegie Hall (also around the corner from Dr. Ricafrente's dental office). There is something inherently fun about staying in a hotel or temporary housing in your hometown. You experience a different part of the city. Different neighborhood, different bodegas, different subway lines.

The only thing better than having this new experience was sharing it. On several occasions I invited my close girlfriends to stay with me and enjoy this corporate housing with me. However many sleepovers I missed in my childhood, I more than made up for in my single twenties. Between May and Alexis, and my college and post-college friends Kristen, Bianca, Tanya, and Melissa, there was no shortage of girls in the rotation. One night, I invited some of them to come over and enjoy the Carnegie Hall neighborhood. This happened to be during the height of Hurricane Rita,

My girlfriends as my bridesmaids in 2009. Weddings became a different story with kids in 2014.

which was moving toward the Texas Gulf Coast. Weather reports dominated cable news and we had CNN on in the background as we caught up over Chinese take-out and put on our facemasks.

As Anderson Cooper showed a shot of the evacuation route, Kristen commented, "My friend Nicole thinks Anderson Cooper is really hot ..."

"Hmm ..." I looked toward the television and looked at him closely. "I guess he's good looking ..."

Kristen wanted a second opinion. "What do you think of Anderson Cooper, May?"

May looked a little confused and smiled sheepishly. "Hmm ... who's Anderson Cooper?"

Now Kristen and I were confused. "Umm ... the guy who's been on TV since you got here..."

"Ahh ..." she started giggling.

"Why, what's so funny?" I asked.

"Nothing, nothing ..." May responded but couldn't stop with the silly grin.

"I don't get it ..." Kristen looked at me.

I shrugged in agreement. "C'mon ... what is it, May?" I pleaded for her to let us in on her joke.

"Okay, fine, but don't laugh at me," she sighed and finally gave in. "I thought *he* was 'Rita Strikes.'"

We were totally confused until we looked at the TV and saw "RITA STRIKES" on the screen below Anderson Cooper's face. We still use this story as a remedy for a bad day.

So, You Breathe Oxygen?

Going to the Philippines when we were kids was synonymous with visiting relatives. We would come back from one month in the Philippines and my classmates would expect to hear elaborate descriptions of coconut trees, clear water, and white sand beaches. I could offer none of that.

"Was the sand like talcum powder?"

"I didn't actually spend much time in the sand ..."

"Was the ocean like bath water?"

"I never actually swam at the beach ..."

"Was it as hot as they say it is?"

"I didn't actually play outside ..."

"So what did you actually do there?"

"Mostly visit relatives ..."

They would then turn to another friend and ask, "So, how was Argentina?"

If we weren't visiting relatives on my mother's side, we were visiting relatives on my father's side. And we're not talking my parents' siblings and my first cousins. A trip back to the Philippines meant that we had to see each one of my grandparents' siblings and their families. *Tita* Lydia, *Tita* Fanny, *Tita* Rita, *Tita* Corazon, *Tito* Ernesto, the list went on. In retrospect I can fully appreciate this gesture by my parents, but at the time it wasn't exactly fun.

Meeting up with cousins was easy. Sure, it took a little time to break the ice after several years of not seeing one another, but once that was done we found all sorts of things in common. "Oh, you guys like singing The Jets? Us too!" The Jets were an American family band composed of brothers and sisters. Their 1980s hit singles like "Crush on You" and "Make It Real" tugged at our easy listening and R&B heartstrings. My friend, Kristen, would say that our family would be The Jets if only my parents had more kids. In our Filipino circles, we had a theory that the band must have Filipino roots somewhere in their Hawaiian blood, but as it turns out they are from the South Pacific island kingdom of Tonga.

The hardest part was sitting through multiple meals and *meriendas* with generation after generation, especially when conversation didn't naturally flow. One time in particular, we were visiting one of my father's relatives, and after the first hour of pleasantries and small talk there was nothing left to say. My father can talk to anybody about anything, however, so this was not a problem for him. He had resorted to asking about the fish in the small aquarium behind the sofa. "How often do you need to feed the fish? Do you need to feed some fish more often than others or do they generally eat at the same time?" When he exhausted all possible questions about the fish, he then moved on to the stray dogs barking outside the house. "Do they wake you up at night? Are they calmer during the day? Do you benefit from them chasing away cats?" Topics of animals didn't limit him, though. He could hold a conversation about the floor. "Is this the original wood? How do you protect it from the humidity? Can you just sweep it with a regular broom or do you sometimes need to use a mop?"

At one point Justin leaned over and said, "So ... do you breathe oxygen?"

We both got the church giggles—and a disapproving look from our father.

Health Class and Mrs. Galvez

To say I was naïve when I first moved to New York would be an understatement. I must have worn my terrified expression as we walked the streets of New York because, as my *Tito* Francis would say, I was a magnet for crazy people. There was one time when we walked out of a movie theater across from Bloomingdales in midtown Manhattan and a homeless man jumped in front of my face, screaming, "WHO FRAMED ROGER RABBIT?" I tried not to make eye contact but he was enjoying my fright. "DON'T LOOK THE OTHER WAY. I SAID, 'WHO FRAMED ROGER RABBIT?!?'" I was probably the only kid who had nightmares about this friendly and talkative white bunny.

Everything was a shocker to me my first year or so in New York City, including Health class. I was under the impression that this hour every other week would complement PE. Little did I know that this session was pretty much just an excuse for twelve-year-old students to talk about sex. After all, it had only been a year, if that, since I had learned about how babies were conceived.

My cousin Natasha had been talking about the birds and the bees in passing when I stopped her.

"Wait, wait. What did you just say?" I had asked with disbelief.

My poor cousin looked horrified. She did her nervous laugh. "You know how babies are made, right?" My blank expression answered her question. She didn't know what to do at this point but explain to me how conception works. "The man has to put his ..." she proceeded to describe.

And to this day, Natasha still remembers my response: "Are you sure? I don't think my mother would ever do that!"

It's a good thing Natasha gave me that lesson when she did, because fast forward a few months later and I was getting much more explicit details from my classmates in Health class.

In typical goody-two-shoes style, I shared this with my parents over dinner and they too were a little surprised by how much I picked up in the short time we had been in New York. They didn't get too worked up—I guess they figured at some point I would have to learn about this—but my mother still checked with her fellow Filipina colleague who worked in the PE department of the Middle School. Lulu Galvez had taught at International School Manila (ISM) where my mother had worked before she and my father migrated to Canada. *Tita* Tessie, Mrs. Galvez, and my mother were all former ISM teachers who were now teaching at UNIS.

"You know, Lulu, Claire mentioned that in her Health class they talk a lot about sex ..." My mother said on the drive home one day. We often carpooled with Mrs. Galvez and her kids.

"Oh, that's normal, Nore. They need to learn some time ..." Mrs. Galvez replied as she merged onto FDR Drive.

"Even about ..." and then she softly whispered, "blowjob?"

Mrs. Galvez turned her head to look at my mother, "What's that?"

On a budget trip to Cancun as new college grads. We couldn't stop laughing when we saw our airline's sign was taped up to the wall.

Deep Thoughts by Claire Lim

*A*LONG WITH HUMOROUS VIGNETTES OF FAMILY AND FRIENDS, my memory is also filled with stray observations I've made over the years. Saturday Night Live used to include short segments between sketches when a voice would say, "And now, Deep Thoughts by Jack Handey ..." as peaceful easy listening music would play and someone, presumably Jack Handey, would read the Deep Thought as the text to it scrolled across the screen. I can almost hear this voice as I have the following thoughts.

TV Observations ...

Oscar *Winners Never Thank God,* Grammy *Winners Always Do*

I've always loved awards shows, especially the music ones. When we were kids, my best friend Henny and her sisters, Amy and Bet, would tape *The Grammys* and every other music awards show on their VCR and we would watch replays of our favorite performances. We must have seen the Jackson Five reunion at *The 10th Annual American Music Awards* a few hundred times. We didn't grow up watching too many movies (this turns out to be the case with many minorities and immigrant families, I've noticed), so the *Academy Awards* mainly interested me for the fashion. One difference between the two, I've always noticed, is that *Grammy* winners almost always start by thanking God and *Oscar* winners never do. In fact, most *Oscar* winners make no mention of God. In the past, I've wondered if this was a racial thing. Most *Oscar* winners are white. Many *Grammy* winners are black. But then, even the white country singers thank God. Is there something about music that makes you spiritual? Maybe. I haven't figured this one out but always thought it would make for a good sociology thesis.

Afterschool Specials

I've admitted before that I'm a little old fashioned. I've always been a bit of a prude but, especially now, seeing things through the lens of my children I cringe watching MTV videos like "Booty" by Jennifer Lopez and Iggy Azalea, and don't even get me started on "Bound 2" by Kanye West. When I was growing up, the most adult content you would see on network TV was Afterschool Specials. These were made-for-TV movies that dealt with controversial or socially relevant issues. They were targeted at teenagers and broadcast at 4:00 p.m. Now I find myself wondering, whatever happened to them? They seem to have gone the way of other old daytime TV favorites like soap operas. I will never forget how crushed I felt a few years ago when ABC announced they would be cancelling *All My Children* and *One Life to Live*, both of which ran for over forty years. To this day, they bring back warm memories of my grandmothers who would take turns covering my eyes during love scenes.

Immigrant and Ethnic Group Observations ...

Asian Eyes

It was on a trip to Cancun with my friends, Kristen, Tanya, May, and Alexis, when I first truly observed the difference between how Asian and Caucasian people get out of the water. My Asian girlfriends Kristen, Tanya, and May all did as I did. After lifting our heads out of the water, we wiped our face down with the palm of one of our hands. Hardly the pool scene from *Fast Times at Ridgemont High*. Alexis, on the other hand, looked effortlessly glamorous. She's half Greek and half Jewish, and she has those lashes every girl wants. She emerged from the water and batted her beautiful eyes as tiny drops settled on her long dark lashes. She might as well have been Phoebe Cates.

This observation was recently validated by my four-year-old son Carlos. He had forgotten his goggles during one swimming lesson so he was telling me that he couldn't swim as well that day. "I get it, Carlos. It's hard to see underwater without your goggles," I said empathetically.

"Actually, the problem isn't when I'm underwater," he explained. "The problem is whenever I have to lift my head out of the water I need to wipe my eyes." And just like that he validated a theory my Asian girlfriends and I have had for the last fifteen years.

Minorities Don't Know Movies

I can't tell you how many times I get that shocking look of disbelief that accompanies questions like, "You've never seen *The Godfather?*" "What about *Casablanca?*" "These are classics!" At some point I started observing that this didn't only happen to me but also to my other second-generation immigrant friends.

I recently read a study validating that people with lower incomes participate at lower rates in a wide range of activities, including not just classical music concerts and plays but also forms of engagement that would be considered less "elitist," like going to the movies.[7] Maybe immigrant and minority parents couldn't afford to go to the movies. Maybe they didn't have time to hang out and watch movies. Maybe they didn't like the way they were portrayed in them. Or maybe we're just not ashamed to admit we haven't watched them. Separately, I came across another survey that found four out of five people lie about having seen films to impress others.[8]

Food and Snack Observations ...

Pringles

The Pringles cylinder patent must have expired. Has anyone else out there wondered why all of a sudden almost every chipmaker now has a line of chips that comes in the long cylinder containers once associated solely with Pringles? Lays, Mr. Potato, Mr. Tomas, and many more.

Nerds

Nerds have come back in a big way: Nerds were one of those candies that were HUGE in the 1980s. Their unique container with two flavors per box took candy to a new level. Justin and I could make one box of Nerds last a year. I didn't hear much about them for what seemed like decades but now all of a sudden there are all these spin offs: Sour Nerds, Giant Chewy Nerds, Jumbo Nerds, etc.

---

[7] Createquity, "Why Don't They Come?"
[8] *The Guardian*, "Four out of five tell The Godfather of all lies about seeing classic films"

Chiclets

Do Chiclets still exist? Outside of Latin America? Every once in a blue moon I see them in a Walgreens or a Halloween bag but their popularity certainly decreased since my childhood.

Baby Sofia's baptism in Manila coincided with Pope Francis' recent papal visit to the Philippines

Making the Best of Everything

"The happiest people don't have the best of everything,
they just make the best of everything." – Unknown

Outside All Saints Parish with the Rebodos family

Everything is Funnier at Church

FROM EARLY ON, MY BROTHER AND I picked up on our parents' cues and made the most of every situation. We took literally my mother's reminder that we were too smart and creative to ever be bored. We added our own color to even the most monotonous occasions, including church (sorry, Mom).

We could have written a book about how to keep ourselves entertained at church. Every Sunday as we were growing up in Vancouver, we would go to mass at All Saints Parish, which was just a ten-minute drive from our house in Coquitlam. We never complained about going, especially since it was actually bonus time to see family and friends. My childhood best friend Henny and her family were regulars at our mass. So were our cousins, Natasha, Faisal, and Walid, along with *Tita* Nori. Then there were the Linos, the Mendozas, and several other Filipino families. We often ended up going to someone's house right after church for an impromptu lunch. On special days we might eat out somewhere like Penny's, a hole in the wall Chinese restaurant on East Hastings where the food was tasty and plentiful.

Aside from daydreaming about delicious Cantonese pan-fried noodles that could be a mere hour away, one way to keep mass interesting was to make up little games. Our favorite was "Guess which psalm?" referring to which psalm the choir was going to sing during the Liturgy of the Eucharist. The Sunday Missal gave a choice during this section:

> (Priest) Let us proclaim the mystery of faith:
> (All) Christ has died, Christ is risen,
> Christ will come again.
> or
> Dying you destroyed our death,
> rising you restored our life.
> Lord Jesus, come in Glory.
> or
> When we eat this bread and drink this cup, we proclaim your
> death, Lord Jesus, until you come in Glory.
> or
> Lord, by your cross and resurrection you have set us free.
> You are the Savior of the world.

It gave us great delight if we guessed the right hymn seconds before the choir sang it. We would pump our elbows and do a big "Yesssss!" gesture (silently, of course) and you would think we had just learned that we won Lotto 6/49 (one of two national lottery games in Canada).

My brother and I quickly learned that you can't underestimate the importance of music in a mass. There was the 9:00 a.m. no-music mass (this had its advantages because you were guaranteed a speedy service), the 10:30 a.m. mass with the three folk singer sisters complete with guitars (our favorite), or the 12:00 p.m. high mass with a full choir singing choral music (beautiful but not the most fun for singing along). The folk singer sisters sang the Catholic Church greatest hits: "Eagle's Wings," "Be Not

One of many CLC gatherings

Afraid," "Here I Am, Lord," and "One Bread, One Body." My friend Kristen and I often refer to these as the church songs you'd want at your wedding or (pardon the morbidity) memorial service. Anyone who grew up going to a Catholic church knows these are classics.

We were at mass a few months back and I was reminded about the power of "Here I Am, Lord." The church we were attending in Singapore has consistently long masses every Sunday. If it hadn't been literally steps away from our condo we would have probably started going to another church. The priest at this church is what my husband Alex calls an "Old Testament priest." In technical terms, the Old Testament refers to the first section of the Christian bible, it was written mostly in Hebrew, and it takes you through everything that happened before Jesus. For many, the Old Testament is associated with a God of wrath and the New Testament a God of love. Old Testament Priest may mean well but he spends more time criticizing behavior of people in church instead of making them feel welcome.

Sometimes it actually felt like Old Testament Priest was purposely trying to make us stay in church as long as possible. Usually the homily is the one variable of the mass because priests' sermons can be as long or as short as they feel like on any given week. The rest of the mass is pretty predictable. At this church, we had the unknown length of time for the homily *plus* the unknown addition to the mass. Typically, after the homily, everyone stands up and we move on to the Liturgy of the Eucharist, otherwise known as the final stretch. Not with Old Testament Priest. He likes to throw "extras" into his services. This could mean celebrating every couple who had a wedding anniversary that month with a special blessing, it could mean bringing out everyone converting to Catholicism for the parishioners to bear witness, or it could mean having a nun come up to share her experience in Uganda. All wonderful things but, when they come unexpectedly between everyone and lunch, it could get painful. For most parents, it means keeping already restless children more entertained. For many women, it means sending apologetic looks and shrugs to their reluctant but supportive husbands.

You can imagine then that when the end of mass finally comes and the final hymn is sung, parishioners practically push their way out of the door. Alas, not with "Here I Am, Lord." This song keeps everyone, my husband included, in their pews until the last verse.

We've been fortunate to have a number of New Testament priests in our lives. Shortly after my family moved to New York, my parents became a part of Christian Life Community (CLC). By definition, CLC is an international association of lay Christians who have adopted an Ignatian (Jesuit) model of spiritual life. In practice, it just felt like a group of my parents' closest Filipino friends in the tri-state area (the Centeneras, the Jongcos, the Custodios, the Velos, and the Santos') getting together with a great down-to-earth priest, Father Dan Fitzpatrick. Every other weekend they got together in one of their homes, reflected on a topic previously agreed upon, had mass, and then ate like it was nobody's business. The meetings were supposed to last one and a half or two hours but, for this group, it was an all-day social affair complete with an all-out Filipino food spread. As the years went by, Justin and I also became close with the other "CLC kids" including Kristen and her siblings, Melissa and Robert. Soon CLC meetings became synonymous with karaoke, Guitar Hero, and the popular board game Sequence.

When it was my parents' turn to host, I couldn't help but overhear the discussion. The idea of a Christian prayer group can sometimes conjure images of crazy religious fanatics but this was anything but that. This was an intimate chat between close friends reflecting on areas in which they found strength and discomfort, and ultimately how they could each be better people. They also focused on how to serve the poor. If Pope Francis had a prayer group, this would be it. They're on social media as much as he is, they have adopted Jesuit spirituality as he has, and they smile as much as he does.

In general, whenever people (especially from our generation and non-Filipinos) hear that Alex and I go to church every Sunday they are surprised. Most of my second-generation Filipino cousins and friends don't go regularly and I get it. Many of them are in inter-faith relationships; many no longer identify so much with the Catholic Church. In my case, I like going to church as a family. I like having the built-in time to reflect and be grateful for everything. I like the discipline that comes with going every Sunday. I like the fact that while we all may not feel like doing it, we all rally and go. I like that my young kids have to learn to sit through something that's not inherently fun. And I like looking forward to the family activity that follows. I don't know if these are all the right reasons to go to church but there you have it. I'm incredibly grateful to Alex for being supportive of this practice. It's the last thing he wants to do on Sunday morning and I fully appreciate that.

When we were kids, one of the first things Justin and I would do when we were seated was look at the hymn board that had all the page numbers of the songs that would be sung during that mass. We would quickly flip to all these pages in the hymnal

Guitar Hero in the Jongcos' basement

and if any of the classics were on there, it was going to be a good day! The rest of the mass would be spent practicing harmonies and second voice to the choir's first voice. This could get embarrassing if people in the row before or behind us took notice and gave us the "Who are these weirdos?" expressions but we paid no mind.

My mother will probably cringe when she reads this church passage but she'll find some comfort in knowing that some of my fondest memories are in church or are church related. Like the time Justin had his first religious revelation. He was around ten years old when he started asking about the difference between Catholics and Protestants.

"Mom, what's the difference between our church and this church?" Justin asked as we drove by an Episcopalian parish.

My mother's go-to answer on this one was the presence of Christ in Holy Eucharist. That is, Catholics believe that the bread and wine change into the actual body and blood of Christ whereas Protestants believe that Christ is present in spirit, but the bread and wine are merely symbolic.

"So Catholics believe the bread and wine change into the actual body and blood of Jesus and Protestants believe the bread and wine are just a symbol?" Justin wanted to clarify.

"Yes, that's right," my mother answered. As he said it aloud, I could see where this was going and hoped my mother was prepared.

"Umm ... I think I'm Protestant ..." Justin said a few seconds later. By this time I was laughing because it sounded reasonable enough but my mother was not as amused.

With family priests Father Dan Fitzpatrick and Father Erno Diaz

New Year's Eve dinner party

WHY ARE YOU ALWAYS SO DRESSED UP?

*P*ART OF LIVING YOUR BEST IS LOOKING YOUR BEST. I was always one of those people who was asked, "Why are you so dressed up?" This was especially true in college. I don't know if it was the case everywhere but at Yale if you bothered to shower and wash your hair, you were stepping up your game. If you put on make-up or wore anything from Banana Republic or Express, the assumption was that Proctor and Gamble or McKinsey was in town for campus recruiting. This is no longer the case, by the way. I recently went back to Yale to speak at an event hosted by the Yale Women's Leadership Initiative and I couldn't help but notice that many of the students dressed more stylishly than I remember. Some of them were also taking Uber cars to class, so clearly a number of things have changed.

In my case, I soon began to realize that if I did see someone who looked dressed up in college, there was a 50 percent chance she was from New York City, a 30 percent chance she was from another US city (most likely LA, San Francisco, Chicago, Boston, DC, or Miami) and a 20 percent chance she was an international student. And this wasn't just true for the girls. Apparently "city guys" had a certain look as well. "They're pretty boys who use gel in their hair and wear colors like salmon," I remember my roommate Stephanie saying. They also shopped at places like Structure (the male equivalent of Express), which meant they were trying to be "all GQ."

The backhanded compliment was all too common. "Wow, someone looks nice! I can't even find the time to wash my hair ..." But I was never pressured into dressing down. I remained the shameless girl who put on lip-gloss before going to the gym. Hoops at the beach. Oh, and I got dressed up when sick. In this regard, I was practically a Kardashian.

But alas, there came a turning point in life when dressing up became a positive, even enviable thing (kind of like hanging out with your parents). Dressing up meant you were "put together," which meant you were highly competent.

My family and I recently moved to Hong Kong. On my first day of work, I came to the office early and waited in the reception area until one of the assistants arrived.

"Hi, let me see if I can find out where you'll be sitting," she said helpfully as she flipped through some files. "You're in an office, right?"

"I don't know actually," I responded. Offices are becoming few and far between and since I was just being transferred I wasn't making any assumptions.

"You look like you would have an office," she commented, smiling.

I smiled back. While there are obviously more substantial factors, you should never underestimate the importance of perception.

There are a few simple things that make me feel "put together ..."

Big Accessories

One thing I've noticed about women in corporate America is the bigger the job, the bigger the accessories. I used to think I would never use any of the big jewelry pieces that my mom or her sister, *Tita* Lynn, generously gave me. At the time they seemed gigantic and clunky. Now I find myself frantically looking for these precious pieces because I know that along with a strong and dynamic presentation they'll make a big impact.

Gel Manicures

I used to associate gel manicures with intricate nail art and blinged out designs. Some were pretty, others were downright over the top, but either way I never thought they were appropriate for the workplace. I don't know why it took me so long to realize you could have a simple and classy nail color that takes no time to dry and lasts for weeks without chipping. It's almost too good to be true. They are more expensive than regular polishes but worth the investment, and the put-together perception is huge.

Dry Shampoo

Like many women, my hair can determine whether I'm having a good or bad day. I'm well aware that something so superficial shouldn't hold that much influence on something as significant as my entire day but, hey, I didn't make up the rules. I've only met a handful of women without hair issues. The rest of us have at some point wished for different hair and many of us have taken drastic measures to attain this hair. Whether sitting for four hours through a Japanese straightening process as an adult or doing the economical home perm as an early teen, getting perfect hair is something we grapple with all our lives. A game changer for me has been discovering dry shampoo. I admit this with some caution because I felt slightly ashamed of using this product when I read the label on the back that said something like, "For busy people and bed ridden people ..."

My hair issue has always been about getting more body in it so that it's not flat. I fault my cousin Michelle for this paranoia. One summer, she and the rest of *Tito* Armand's family were visiting us in Vancouver. Michelle was sharing my room and every time she went out she would put in a few hair rollers—not all over her head like the ones Bruno Mars sported in his "Uptown Funk" video. Mainly it was just her bangs. I was around ten years old when I asked her, "Why do you do that?"

"So I don't have flat hair," she answered, putting the last roller in place.

"What is flat hair?" I had no idea.

"It's like ..." she started. "It's like yours ..." she smiled, giving up on any false diplomacy.

Michelle may have brought the whole "hair body" thing to my attention but it was reinforced everywhere I looked in the 1980s. I remember watching a *Three's Company* episode when one of Jack Tripper's girlfriends was bent over brushing her hair upside down. "I'm trying to get some body ..." she explained to Jack, who responded with something cheesy like, "It doesn't look like you need any help with your body!"

Two decades later I discovered dry shampoo. Just in time too, as I was moving to Singapore where my hair would get that much more oily thanks to constant humidity. Dry shampoo absorbs the oil in my hair and leaves it with that highly coveted "body."

Michael Kors Leg Shine

A little bit of a random one. Probably something that others don't notice but it makes me feel more put together (kind of like a subtle perfume). No one wears pantyhose anymore but there was something nice about the smooth silky look a good pair of hose could provide. Michael Kors leg shine is subtle (it doesn't have all the glitter or streaky brown tint that others do) and it has just the right natural sheen.

A Scarf or Pashmina

This accessory is perfect. It's lightweight and takes up no space. It can be tied, draped, or carried. Best of all, it completes any look. I swear, the days I have worn a scarf when I travel, I am upgraded on the plane. If not upgraded, I am made to board first. Or, if not traveling, I am given the window seat at the restaurant.

Mascara

I never had much in the way of lashes but now I realize how much of a difference mascara makes. The first person to point out my sub-optimal lashes was my childhood best friend Henny. We were at the Philippine Carinderia food booth at the Pacific National Exhibition (the PNE in Vancouver, Canada). It was the post-lunch pre-dinner lull when Henny half-jokingly said, "Time to glamorize!" which meant it was time to reapply our makeup.

"Whoa! Your eyelashes go down. You must be stroking your lashes down with the mascara! You're supposed to be stroking up!" she was laughing with condescension.

"I do stroke up!" I said defensively.

"Really? Are you serious?" She said incredulously. "Well, then, your eyelashes are jacked!"

I examined her lashes and indeed they looked totally different from mine. They were thick, they were plenty, and they curled upwards. *Must be her Indonesian side*, I concluded enviously.

When my father came to the PNE later that day, I noticed his lashes looked exactly like mine. Sure, they were long enough. But they were thin, they were fine, and they went straight down.

"Oh man, I got them from you!" I complained before showing him my sad discovery.

"What are you talking about?" He exclaimed. "These are

the best kinds of eyelashes because they shield your eyes from dust and dirt," he concluded with his positive spin.

Because of my lack of lashes, I have learned the impact of mascara. My good friend Kristen and I were once out at a bar where our friend Carmela's sister Liz was bartending. Liz was a model and she looked like one. Kristen and I couldn't help but pepper Liz with compliments and questions, like, "Wow, those are nice shoes ... Where did you get that dress? I love your lipstick ... Are those your real eyelashes?

"I use thirty-five strokes of mascara on each lash," I remember Liz explaining.

That crosses my mind every now and again when I get dressed for a big day and find myself counting strokes. *Thirty more to go.*

Good Shoes

According to Mireille Guiliano in *French Women Don't Get Facelifts*, there are particular "tells" when it comes to a woman's appearance that signify to others how she feels about herself and how she wants to be perceived by the outside world. The first "tell" is a woman's haircut and the other is her shoes. She believes that a woman can wear expensive or inexpensive clothes and as long as she pairs quality shoes with her outfit, she will shine. On the other hand, an amazingly well styled ensemble can be ruined by shabby shoes.[9]

Henny also uses shoes as the litmus test for someone with good taste. "Anyone can have a nice top or even a nice outfit but that doesn't mean they have good taste. They could have just copied the whole outfit on the mannequin. Now, what shoes they pick to go with the outfit, that's when you really know." Henny is now the Senior Director of Merchandising at Aritzia so she knows what she's talking about.

---

[9] This point is nicely summarized in a blog called *The Simply Luxurious Life – refined living on an everyday income.*

Justin and I posing with (not actually riding) Citi Bikes

Jogging with Alex at MacRitchie Reservoir Park in Singapore

FILIPINA WOMEN DON'T GET FAT

HIS ISN'T AT ALL TRUE, BY THE WAY. It's more of a catchy title than anything else (plus I think it subconsciously came to mind after Mireille Guiliano's book *French Women Don't Get Fat*). That said, I have often been asked, "Where does the food go?" This is more of a reference to my appetite rather than my figure (basically, I eat frequently and I'm not huge). While I'm the last person who should be giving physical fitness or nutritional advice, I do have some musings on the matter.

Filipinos are shameless when it comes to commenting on your weight. If you haven't seen a relative in some time you can be sure the first comment he or she will make is about whether you look thinner or "healthier" since they saw you last. The first time I experienced any self-consciousness about weight was when I came back from college after freshman year. I'll never forget how my *Tita* Tessie took me aside and gently said, "All my sons and their girlfriends also put on weight their first year in college. As long as you're conscious, you can lose it."

Holy not subtle, I thought. But we felt close to *Tita* Tessie particularly after she helped us make the transition from

Vancouver to New York. My mother bought *Tita* Tessie's car for her parents when *Tita* Tessie was immigrating to the States. Her son Luis' girlfriend Mona drove me to my SATs in New Jersey. And *Tita* Tessie once told our whole family that we were all putting on weight.

To be fair, we were going through a period when we were eating way too much pound cake. My mother had learned a particularly good recipe from Henny's mother, *Tita* Hetty. Rich, buttery, and moist with just the slightest crisp on the top, it was always a hit. She starting baking this pound cake once a week (usually Sunday afternoon) but as she mastered her technique of folding in the sour cream and sugar, she began whipping out pound cakes any given hour of the day. I would wake up to sweet and buttery smells from the kitchen. I would come home to soft humming sounds of the KitchenAid mixer. We had so much pound cake around the house that Justin and I started using it to make ham and cheese sandwiches. *Tita* Tessie almost had a legal obligation to tell my mother to stop.

Part of the reason I eat so frequently is that I never turn down food. But it's not necessarily because I'm constantly hungry. I mean, sure, I always want a slice of that chocolate cake passed around after everyone sings "Happy Birthday" but usually I'm not craving that plate of durian when it's offered. Still, I always feel compelled to say yes because the truth is it makes people happy when you do. In the same manner, if I come home after having a heavy Italian dinner and my parents offer me coffee and *ensaymada*, I'll be up for it. I know it's just a reason to spend time chatting around the dining table.

Between my genuine appreciation of food and my desire to be social, I eat frequently and I should be exercising regularly but I just can't seem to get into the rhythm. I have watched many of my girlfriends (even those like me who were never particularly athletic) get hooked on some form of physical fitness whether yoga or pilates, running or Soul Cycle. They have found their "thing" and incorporated it into their life, which has given them more balance. I try to run with my husband on the weekends but it's not quite the same. Writer and actor Mindy Kaling recently said in an interview, "I have to pretend, when I run, that I'm avenging the murder of, like, my husband …" and this actually resonated with me.

I'll always remember how shocked my girlfriends in Miami were to learn that I didn't own socks. Olga and Jackie were helping me pack up boxes when I was getting ready to move them back to New York.

"Okay, give me all the socks you've got," Olga said in her take-charge way. "I'll use them as a buffer for all your fragile things."

"I don't have socks," I answered.

This made Olga and Jackie burst into laughter.

"Incredible! How can you not own socks?" Jackie asked.

I didn't get why this was hard to understand. "We live in Miami. When do we ever wear socks?"

"Umm … whenever we run or go to the gym or …" And that explained it.

There have been several points in my life when I've thought, "That will make me get in shape." When I moved into

For the Lim family, exercising is so rare it merits a photo session

The Flamingo, the beautiful people party condo on South Beach, I thought, "How can I not start going to the gym here?" Or when I learned I was moving to Brazil and started daydreaming about weekends in Rio, I said, "At least I'll feel the pressure to get toned." Recently I've been seeing friends posting on Facebook about doing marathons or climbing mountains before turning forty and I've thought, *That will be a good reason to start working out regularly.* So far nothing has moved the needle.

Part of it may be that I don't look or feel natural doing physical activity.

"You don't look like yourself. You look like your weird athletic cousin," my friend Alexis once commented as I walked out in new workout gear.

Another time, Kristen and I were visiting our friend Danny in Guadalajara. Danny had become a good friend from Yale and he was in Mexico on an assignment for the US Department of State. The great host that he was, he insisted on driving us up to Puerto Vallarta while we were there. Hours after we arrived, he and his friends took us out on boats and jet skis. It looked like a scene out of a Mexican *Baywatch*. Everyone was beautiful, tanned, and active. After lunch, someone suggested we drive up to the mountains to see the picturesque waterfalls. We parked the jeep and everyone took turns diving into the water and swimming to the other end of the river.

Jogging with Alex and our friend Mari at Parque Ibirapuera in Sao Paulo

Hmm, this will be interesting, I thought. Technically I could swim. I passed every treading test required in school. Heck, I even taught swimming to kindergartners during UNIS summer camp. But I never swam very much distance and I didn't exactly have the breathing and strokes down.

Since I didn't know how to dive, I did one big leap into the water and just went for it. I thought of my father. Fake it 'til you make it. Sometimes when you visualize yourself doing something well, you end up doing it well. This wasn't one of those times. It took all of my will and concentration to get to the other side. I bobbed up for air when necessary and kept moving my arms and legs. I felt quite proud of myself as I reached the other end. That is, until everyone ran toward me asking if I was okay.

"I'm totally fine," I said casually, trying to hide the fact that I was out of breath. "I was just swimming ..."

"That wasn't swimming," Danny shook his head. "That was surviving!"

I knew the jig was up.

I did have one good stretch of running when I first started dating Alex. We were living in Sao Paulo and I'd get calls from him.

"Hey, do you want to go for a run at Ibirapuera before dinner?" Parque Ibirapuera was like the Central Park of Sao Paulo and conveniently it was just down the road from our corporate housing at the Marriott Executive Suites.

"Sure, sounds great!" It actually sounded about as appealing as doing expense reports but he was cute and we were in a good place so I was in. Plus, faking running is much easier than faking swimming.

Alex is the first to point out that as we grew closer together my running aspirations got further away. To this day I still haven't quite figured out nutrition or physical fitness. However, I do have random tips I've picked up to help keep up your appearance and stay in some form of shape ...

Chocolate Malt Balls and M&Ms

I was never one to feel peer pressure when it came drinking, smoking, or any of the other common associations. With food, however, it's a completely different story. I tend to eat whatever my companions eat. There are times when I've been looking over a menu with new colleagues at lunch and salivating over thoughts of the bacon cheeseburger and truffle fries. When the waiter comes around to take the order, however, everyone starts rattling off different kinds of fish and greens.

"I'll have the grilled halibut."

"I'll try the quinoa harvest salad."

"I'll do the sesame crusted tuna."

"The sea bass for me," will be my answer. Sea bass is my default healthy order. It's delicious but I'm always hungry afterward. My mind starts wandering off to how I'll supplement later on. *Maybe I can stop by Chipotle for two soft tacos or I can get a monster cookie from Starbucks.*

My friend Alexis went through what she jokingly refers to as her "anorexic" stage. She had just graduated from Brown and was taking acting classes at The Lee Strasberg Theatre and Film Institute. Alexis was by no means anorexic and we realize it's a very serious disease. She was just eating healthy and going to the gym religiously. She was very particular about her diet so anything she ate was stored away in my head as "good for you" or "won't make you fat." She ate tons of salad, fish, and couscous (this was well before quinoa and kale) so I did too—at least when I was with her. She passed on ice cream but said yes to a Whopper's malted milk ball. "These actually aren't too bad for you," I remember her saying as she pulled out the little milk carton package they came in. Since then I consider malt balls diet food. The same went for a Starbucks vanilla soy latte, which was her go-to order when we hit the coffee shop.

I have similar associations with M&Ms because of actress Kellie Martin, whom I met when we were both students at Yale. Kellie starred in the early 1990s television drama series *Life Goes On* that chronicled the experiences of the Thatcher family including eighteen-year-old son Corky who had Down syndrome. Kellie played Becca, his bookish girl-next-door sister. She was so relatable in this role that by the time I met her in college I felt like I had known her for years already. She was as nice and interesting in person as she was on TV and we became fast friends. We grew closer when we were both tapped as sophomores for the same three-year society at Yale. We spent long Thursday nights together along with a few dozen upperclassmen listening to each other's stories and doing, well, secret society stuff. Kellie was and continues to be a healthy eater but I noticed that she never refused M&Ms when the bowl was passed around. *Note to self, M&Ms can't be that bad*, I established.

Ten-Fry Rule

I also put my former boss Kiane Wallis on the same food pedestal. Tall, pretty, and slender, she looked like a model working at Citibank (her fancy Aussie accent only solidified this idea). She once mentioned in passing that she and her then boyfriend had a ten-fry rule. They could each have ten of the French fries that came with their steak frites before they would stop one another and limit themselves to salad. Still today, ten is the magic number for fries as far as I'm concerned.

Goldfish Crackers

I also try to remember a few facts I've learned along the way. My kids eat a lot of Pepperidge Farm Goldfish Crackers. These things are amazing not just because they're super tasty but also because one serving is fifty-five crackers! It's our family go-to snack.

Leg Lifts While Brushing Teeth

Robin Roberts from *Good Morning America* has mentioned on a couple occasions that she does leg lifts while brushing her teeth. I try to do this whenever I remember. (By the same token, Diane Sawyer says she sings the Happy Birthday song when she washes her hands because that's the appropriate length of time to clean thoroughly. I try to do this too.)

Warm Up Your Food

My former boss Pat Raufer always heated up her lunch even if it was just served at the canteen. "You're eating the calories anyway. Might as well fully enjoy them," she would say.

Say No to Mediocrity

I always remember the time Alex and I were at our friend Danny's house party on the Lower East Side and my friend Yara offered him a bowl of Bugles. Bugles are a corn chip snack food named after their "bugle" (musical horn) shape. We had all been commenting on how hungry we were since we had only eaten a light dinner that evening so she was surprised when he declined. "Really? I thought you were so hungry ..."

"Not for that salty cone of mediocrity," he replied as we all burst into laughter. His description was spot on and we got the point. If you don't derive real satisfaction from it, just pass. (Bugles have been discontinued in many countries due to decrease in demand, by the way.)

Cut It In Half

Before you start digging into your meal, cut it in half. As prudent immigrants, my parents did this all the time when we were eating out at a restaurant (not so much at family gatherings where there was an abundance of food). Whatever dish you ordered while you were out was going to be shared. More often than not, you don't even miss the second half.

Eat Sitting Down

Who knew I would be referencing Mireille Guiliano so often in this book? I remember taking away this piece of advice from *French Women Don't Get Fat*. She gives a number of helpful tips but to eat while sitting down particularly resonated with me because it also underlined the importance of enjoying every moment and savoring every bite.

Wait Five Minutes

While I was working in Manila, I became friends with a former model and Philippine beauty queen, Tina Pamintuan. Tina taught me a bunch of modeling tricks like how to take photos from a high angle so they're more flattering. She also showed me her secret for portion control. Tina was a foodie so she appreciated a good meal. We were eating the most delicious piece of steak and when someone offered her a second serving, she said, "I'm going to wait five minutes to see if I still want it ..." I would follow her lead when I was with her and, amazingly, each time I didn't need it afterward.

A Word About McDonald's

Also engrained in my mind now is the fact that a McDonald's cheeseburger is actually only 290 calories. I came across a headline recently that read, "11 surprising foods with way more calories than a McDonald's cheeseburger." A medium movie theater

With the Rebodos kids in a McDonalds hamburger tower

Carlos was drawing McDonalds French Fries at the age of three

Road Trip Pringles Party

Let's just say we have fun with fast food...

popcorn (1,610 calories) is equivalent to five and a half McDonald's cheeseburgers! A few other fun facts from this Vox article's "The Cheeseburger Conversion Chart" are that one pecan crusted chicken salad at TGIFriday's is the equivalent of three and a half cheeseburgers while one grilled turkey toasted sandwich at Chili's is equivalent to four and a half cheeseburgers.

I'm not ashamed to admit that my family and I have always had a soft spot for McDonald's. Alex often jokes that we could make a counter movie to *Super Size Me*. When we were living in Singapore, there was a McDonald's too conveniently located in the Great World City shopping mall across the street from our condo. During those four years, our family must have stopped by McDonald's a couple times a week. Sometimes we would all share one order of large fries and a chocolate sundae. Other times, we would "family style" two value meals.

Aside from frequency of visits, there are a few other indications that you're serious fans of McDonald's:

1. My parents would have to distract me in the car if they saw the golden arches coming up. Apparently I would cry my eyes out if we drove past one. I'm a little ashamed to admit that we kind of do this with my daughter now.

2. Justin and I actually gave a name to the delightful fries left at the bottom of a McDonald's bag: surfries.

3. A McDonald's trip alone was enough to get Justin out of bed at 10 p.m. Whenever my father wanted company on a drive he would dangle the McDonald's carrot (that sounds like an oxymoron, I know). I went home one weekend in college and my family was kind enough to drive me back to New Haven from New York. Shortly after they left, however, I realized that I had forgotten a notebook that had all the information I needed to review for a midterm. "No problem," my dad said. "I can drive back." My father would always be up for a road trip especially if that meant more time

with family. "Hey, Justino," I heard him call out, "you want some McDonald's?"

4. We have been trick or treating at McDonald's. When we were little kids in Vancouver, we would go from McDonald's to McDonald's availing of their "trick or treat" special whereby they would give one hamburger to every child who came through their door. I'm sure McDonald's headquarters did the math, assuming that each family would end up buying a couple more sets of burgers, fries, and soft drinks for the parents, at least fries and a drink for the kid, etc. They did not account for families like mine who drove to every McDonald's in town, grabbing the burgers and nothing else. My family has more than made up for this through our lifelong loyalty.

5. I have sent back McDonald's. The other day Alex and I went for a long walk and we ended up at McDonald's (shocker). When it's just the two of us we'll usually just stop in for a large diet coke and a chocolate sundae. On this particular afternoon Alex went to the restroom and left me to order. I used this as a chance to throw in a small order of French fries. I was still waiting to pay the tab when I took a bite of one of the fries sitting on the tray. Immediately I knew I had drawn the short end of the fry (so to speak). This must have been the tail end of fries from the last batch sitting in the food warmer. I sent it back and asked if I could get the new fries. Did you know it only takes three minutes to wait for a whole new batch of fries? It takes five to ten minutes for Starbucks to brew a new pot of coffee.

On a scenic run in Singapore

My swimming challenge on the trip to Puerto Vallarta

Only my husband can get me to sign up for organized runs

Dressing up for Isabel's birthday dinner at home

CLAY ANIMATION
(AND OTHER THINGS THAT LOSE ME)

*A*LEX OFTEN GIVES ME A HARD TIME about what we watch for entertainment. "It has to be a Lim wheelhouse movie," he explains to others, "which basically means it has to have Kevin James in it, or it has to be TV." (Ever since that one time he clicked on my DVR recordings and saw nothing but old episodes of *King of Queens* he won't stop with the Kevin James jokes. Justin's constant references to the movie *Paul Blart: Mall Cop* probably don't help.)

Plus, he's witnessed firsthand that there are few things that get me more excited than the Fall season premieres of my favorite programs. The updated clips that accompany the theme songs, the new hairstyles the main characters sport (the "lob" has been especially popular during recent seasons), the weight gains or losses (no one fluctuated more than Chandler on *Friends*). It's amazing how much can change between seasons.

But this doesn't mean I don't like movies. I'll admit that some films (especially those in black and white and technicolor) tend to lose me. At one point I rationalized that it was because these movies were typically watched at home so I wasn't completely focused. But the truth is the same thing happens even when I'm at the theater for certain movies (usually ones with overall grey coloring like *Lord of the Rings: The Two Towers* when most of the film takes place in caves), stories about medieval times (probably related to the first "grey hue" issue), and science fiction (unless there's a huge non-science fiction component to the storyline like the TV series *LOST* where a good chunk of each show was sci-fi-free flashbacks). When I was a kid, I had the same issue with clay animation. No matter how much I loved Christmas specials, I just zoned out once *Rudolph* or any other deformable characters came on the screen.

Years ago, Justin and I were in the movie theater watching *Gangs of New York*, an epic historical drama set in the mid-nineteenth century. There was one scene where Cameron Diaz was getting dressed in front of a mirror and Justin turned to me and whispered, "Soak this up, Claire. This is as good as it's gonna to get for you." According to him, I only like movies with makeover scenes à la *Pretty Woman* and *Clueless*. This isn't necessarily true. I also have a penchant for movies that, no surprise, tell immigrant stories from any group and genre, from *My Big Fat Greek Wedding* to *Slumdog Millionaire* to *Life is Beautiful*.

So, to summarize, movies I get excited about watching:

1. Romantic comedies (almost goes without saying).
2. Movies that have a wedding storyline (huge overlap with number one).
3. Movies that focus on an ethnic group (Irish cop movies count, so do many foreign films).

And I guess that it's it. Well, maybe the Kevin James thing was only a slight exaggeration.

Whenever we do have plans to watch a movie that doesn't fall into one of the three categories above, I ask myself, "How can I enjoy this?" or "What can I do to make this fun?" I then suggest we get a fun snack beforehand or I choose a theater in a neighborhood I'll enjoy walking around afterward. The AMC Loews Lincoln Square on 68th and Broadway was typically my favorite.

Big Nick's Pizza Joint was just a couple blocks down around the corner. And as if that weren't enough, Magnolia Bakery (famous for its cupcakes and banana pudding) eventually opened across the street.

I try to do this not just for movies but for anything I'm not looking forward to doing. For instance, when I first started traveling on business I didn't realize how much I would hate doing expense reports. The itemizing of charges, the photocopying of receipts, there was always something more important that needed to get done before such tedious tasks. Then I realized how important it was to submit these reports right away (late fees, potential negative impact to your credit report, etc.) and it became something I couldn't avoid. To motivate myself to make time for expense reports, I started making a night of them. I would choose one day of the week to stay late, order delivery from my favorite Japanese sushi place, and knock out the expense reports. This way they weren't such a chore and part of me looked forward to doing them.

Alex has picked up this approach for me as well. He knows I don't exactly enjoy exercise so when we do long walks or runs over the weekend we often couple them with a refreshing beverage and bite afterward at someplace fun and new that we haven't tried. This actually inspired an article I wrote for Sassy Mama called, "Top 5 Adventure Walks (with Eats) for Families in Singapore." In it, I describe how Alex started looking into outdoor walks for our family. We combined mini hikes with leisurely lunches off the beaten path.

The positive message I see every time I step off the elevator in our Hong Kong office

Living Your Best Life ...
At Work

Arriving at the 2015 APEC Women and the Economy Summit in the Philippines

BAU VS. DWYL

ONE AREA WHERE PEOPLE GENERALLY NEED HELP LIVING their best life is at work. Between *Office Space*, *The Office*, and *Horrible Bosses*, there is no shortage of parodies about the monotony of corporate life. While they are admittedly hilarious, nailing the multitude of acronyms and overused buzzwords, you definitely don't want your life to imitate this art.

Before I go further, let me preface that the following section will likely resonate more with people who work in a corporate setting. Entrepreneurs, consultants, and work-at-home professionals have their own set of challenges (less structure, unpredictable days, not to mention irregular paychecks), but staying motivated is usually not one of them. Speaking from my past experience as well as discussions with friends who are independent professionals, it's easy to stay inspired because you have a vested interest in everything you do. Sure there are frustrating days, but they're building their own brand, their own business, their own relationships. In many cases, they're doing what they love.

Those who work in a corporate setting, on the other hand, have to find ways to stay inspired (by nature, they don't have as much skin in the game). They have to carve out time to do things for themselves, for their own development and their own growth. They need to learn how to invest in themselves. It's easy to get lost (and too comfortable) in a big organization. It's easy to clock in, but also easy to lose motivation.

I read an interview with Richard Branson when he was asked what daily activities he finds motivating and inspiring. He responded, "On Monday, I went out to the Mojave Desert to watch Virgin Galactic, our space tourism company, complete its first rocket-powered flight—it was a truly awesome sight. I treasure such moments, when my team and I find ways to make the impossible possible, inspiring ourselves and others to attempt even greater feats."

Richard Branson is one of those iconic larger-than-life figures. His vision is disruptive, his management style is innovative, his execution is (usually) flawless. But not everyone is able to go out to the Mojave Desert to witness a rocket-powered flight of their team's own creation, and if you read his interview to try to get motivated, it may actually do the opposite. You might come away feeling a little uninspired about your daily life. Instead of looking forward to your team building outing this Thursday, bowling and karaoke may suddenly sound depressingly cliché.

This year marked fourteen years for me at Citi and I have to admit that there's a part of me that winces a little inside whenever someone congratulates me on this anniversary (thank you, LinkedIn). It's not that I don't take pride in working at Citi (far from it, as anyone who knows me will tell you) but nobody wants to be known as a "lifer." Okay, nobody born after the 1960s wants to be known as a "lifer." Sure, at one point, everyone might have aspired for that gold watch symbolizing loyalty and long service. Nowadays, however, job-hopping is the new normal and it's often considered more exciting to have various companies on your resumé. This has come to mean you're aggressive in your career, you're not afraid to take risks, and you're constantly pushing yourself. I never imagined being at Citi for as long as I have been but what I can say, between fourteen years, eighteen bosses, and forty countries, so far it hasn't gotten old.

Still, it holds true that the longer you're with an organization, the more comfortable you get and the more conscious you need to be about staying inspired. In 1999, one of my best friends, Sheldon Gilbert, convinced me to leave American Express to join former classmates from Yale who were starting an Internet company called MagicBeanStalk. Sheldon and I had actually met in high school when he attended one of the student conferences my classmates and I organized at the United Nations. He was young, smart, and passionate. I will always remember how he got up on stage and made a rousing speech about changing the world. For us seventeen-year-olds, it was like watching Barack Obama during the 2004 Democratic National Convention. Sheldon had this way of making you ask yourself what you were going to do to make an impact on earth. Even when he visited me in Miami, he could quickly move the conversation from what's the hottest club in South Beach today to how are you going to save the world tomorrow. He came out with me to dinner one night and I overheard him doing his thing with someone I assumed could care little about anything besides what party we were going to that night. A few minutes after talking to Sheldon, she looked completely introspective and said, "You're right, I *have* to find my passion."

Sheldon wasn't just passionate about saving the world; he was equally passionate about doing things right. Whether he was taking the MCATs or hosting a party, he was intent on flawless execution. We became partners in crime when it came to planning events for our friends. Maybe because I didn't get to socialize so much in my early teens, by the time I was able to go out freely with friends I wanted each time to be an experience. I built up outings in my head based on what I had seen in TV sitcoms. I thought all groups of friends should have their regular diner hangout, perform a lip-synched dance number for a talent show, and work at a country club over summer break. This is what friends did according to *Saved by the Bell*, *90210*, or any number of TV series that featured a group of high school friends.

To my delight, Sheldon had similar ideas. We would talk about doing something fun during the Christmas season and, before long, the two of us had organized ice skating at Central Park, family dinner and Secret Santa gifts by the fire, and delivering Christmas presents to a children's hospital. I knew Sheldon and I were meant to be friends when he created a scavenger hunt around New York City to say thank you to his friends for, well, being great friends. During this scavenger hunt, we went everywhere from Chez Es Saada, a popular new Moroccan restaurant in an old basement cellar (hint: "Even when I'm at the bottom") to the Marriott Marquis (hint: "You make me feel like I'm on top of the world"). A white limo then picked us up and drove us all around the city. We ended at the popular nightclub called Life (where new basketball player Kobe Bryant could often be found along with Puff Daddy and Mike Tyson). Life was also the answer to the final hint: "It would mean nothing without you."

The fact that it was Sheldon who convinced me to join an Internet startup was pretty ironic, because amongst our friends it was a running joke that Sheldon was light years behind on technology. He was the only one in college who never embraced email. He was the last person to get a cell phone. But there we were, two years after he graduated, and he was speaking passionately about the "dot com revolution" and "MBS" as he affectionately called MagicBeanStalk. The idea of MBS was to connect startup companies to everything they would need to get off the ground, beginning with employees. My friend and MBS co-founder James Gutierrez had mastered the art of the job fair back in college where he had put on several successful recruiting events connecting banks and consulting firms to minority students at Yale. With the number of dot coms sprouting across the country (I've still got the elevator pitch down), we were matching up-and-coming startups with college grads across fifty leading US universities.

When I came on board, there were six of us working out of a loft in Williamsburg across from a Mexican bakery. James' bedroom was to the right of my desk. Sheldon sat in front of me next to the kitchen. It was a big change from the American

Express headquarters in the World Financial Center. So was everything about working for a startup. It took a little while to get used to taking the L train to a "gentrifying" neighborhood, using a 718 telephone number on my business card, and making cold calls without a big recognizable company name. Yet, there was an underlying cool factor in being part of what people were calling the "dot com revolution."

It wasn't long before I embraced the startup life. One of the great things about it was that I went from Business Analyst to Head of Marketing. In this role, I got to lead every aspect of the marketing function from picking our company logo, hiring our PR firm, securing sponsors for our events (I was so proud of myself for nailing Handspring, the only competitor out there to Palm Pilot), and planning our industry parties (which were cleverly called BeanScene). I was going to "Convergence" conferences and exchanging business cards with the likes of Jeff Bezos from Amazon and Steve Case of AOL. These were the pre-Google days when most people were using AOL and CompuServe, and the sound of the dial-up 56k modem was pervasive and exciting.

In less than a year, we were able to raise $5 million in venture capital, recruit a legitimate senior management team, and grow to more than fifty employees with offices in New York and California. Eventually, the Internet bubble burst and we all needed to move on to our next gigs. Some continued down the entrepreneurial path and found even more success. James went on to become a leading social entrepreneur and innovator in lending and financial technology. BusinessWeek even selected James as one of America's most promising social entrepreneurs in 2010 after he started Progreso Financiero and helped pioneer new policies on financial empowerment for lower-income consumers. Sheldon ended up developing his own algorithm and became founder and CEO of Proclivity Systems, the leading provider of solutions that give marketers insight into online consumer behavior.

A number of us went back to banks, consulting groups, and law firms. People are often surprised to hear how I came to work at Citi. It wasn't through Yale Career Services or Citi's

Habitat for Humanity's Jimmy Carter Work Project 2004 in Puebla, Mexico

Citi encouraging work life balance

Participating in The Balance Project interview series

Launching *Don't Forget the Soap* in Canada

Sheldon with good friends Olivia and Jackie in Miami

MagicBeanStalk office at TechSpace Union Square

With Citi women leaders Bea Teh-Tan, Philippine Consumer Business Manager and Heather Cox, Head of Citi FinTech

James (center) and Sheldon (right) at our first *BeanScene* event

With the Citibank Philippines team in 2006

Setting up for one of our last dot com trade shows in 2001

campus recruiting program or even a big headhunter. I got my first job at Citi through Monster.com, one of the largest employment websites in the United States and now the world. I didn't think much of it at the time. After all, I was following all the latest startups and we had our eye on Monster.com (and HotJobs.com) as one of the biggest competitors in the job websites space. But whenever I'm asked how I first joined Citi, people think I'm telling a joke when I tell them the truth. "Get out of here!" is the typical response. "For all your high powered schools and contacts, you're telling me you got your job at Citi through a mass online jobs site?" Yes.

And so I found myself back in the middle of skyscrapers, marble elevators, and office cubicles. Sure, I missed feeling like my own boss and running my own shop but there were advantages to working at a big company again. And I'm not just talking about the unlimited stacks of bond paper by the industrial Xerox machine or the complimentary Swiss Miss packs in the pantry. The big household name on your business card was a powerful tool. So too was the company global directory. *I can send an email right now to Former Secretary of Treasury Bob Rubin if I want to. I don't have to share a hotel room. I can attend any one of these leadership courses. That fancy black car is taking me to the airport.* These were the thoughts constantly running through my mind.

I returned to corporate America with a kick in my step. There was a world of resources at my fingertips and I took nothing for granted. At the end of each week, I actually found myself asking the following questions (yes, more litmus tests):

- Did you have butterflies in your stomach at least once this week? This meant I was pushing myself and doing something outside my comfort zone. For me, it often happened before speaking up during a meeting with seniors, asking a question during a town hall meeting, or doing a presentation;
- Did you have lunch or coffee with someone new? Even for extroverts, it's easier to have a lunch at your desk (especially in a place like New York when this is

the norm; in other countries people tend to go out and have a proper sit down lunch) but if you get into this habit you're missing out on opportunities to connect with other people;

- Did you do something to make someone else more successful this week? This could be an introductory email written for a mentee or volunteering to help out on a time-consuming project for a colleague.

If my answers were yes to these questions, then it was a good week. Hard work, high energy, and meaningful networking paid off. I joined business task forces, I used my Filipino connections to help Citi promote our new online remittance service, and I volunteered to lead teams for Global Community Day. I connected with people in every part of the business and every part of the world. Soon, I was identified as "high potential" and selected for unique leadership opportunities.

Several years later, however, the excitement of a big new company wore off and the "I'm going to run the world" high of a management program faded. Things started to become a little BAU (business as usual). A term commonly used in big organizations, "BAU" refers to the normal execution of standard functional operations. The minute you start catching yourself saying "BAU" on a regular basis, it's a wakeup call that you need to do something to spark up your work life. I don't know when it happened exactly but I started to notice that I was going to lunch and coffee with the same people every day, the awards and training photos and diplomas on my desk were starting to get dated, and my resumé hadn't been updated in a couple of years. I no longer felt like the high-energy person with the extra bounce in her step. It was then that I realized I had to start making a conscious effort to reinvigorate my work life.

Below are some tactical things I started to do, which to this day continue to keep me motivated. Whether you're working at a big company, building your own business, taking time off, or going through transition, some of these ideas may resonate with you.

1. Remind yourself of your goals: it's easier to stay motivated when you see where it's all going. My mother writes her goals down on a yellow legal pad she keeps with her at all times. Mine are on the Evernote app. Putting these goals in writing and reminding yourself about them provides clear direction in your day-to-day life and always makes you feel like you're working toward something meaningful.

2. Make regular checkpoints to track your progress: on a regular basis, I do a quick self-assessment to gauge if I'm making progress toward my big goals. Did I grow my business at the rate I targeted? Did I get in front of the right people to share this progress? Did I focus on the right projects that got me closer to my goals?

3. Reward yourself when you achieve a milestone: rewards for me these days can be a lunch by myself after a successful meeting. A guilt-free salted caramel chocolate cupcake from Sift, a bakery I have just discovered near my office in Hong Kong. It can also mean a new pair of Tory Burch shoes.

4. Keep up with leaders and others who inspire you: read what they're reading (Sheryl Sandberg recommends *A Short Guide to a Happy Life*; Jeff Bezos asks all his senior managers to read *The Effective Executive*). Watch the TED talks they're watching. Don't be too cool for Town Halls. These things remind you to think about how you fit into the whole scheme of things.

5. Say your plans out loud to your family and friends: I know some people who never do this. I realize it's because they never want to disappoint or "fail" at something, but when you put your goals out there you are more likely to achieve them because you put some pressure on yourself. I knew the moment I said, "Yes, I'm writing a second book," that I would get it done.

6. Go to conferences and trainings—get out there: the longer you're inside an organization, the more important it

is for you to get outside. When I was at MagicBeanStalk, going to conferences was integral to my job. I've learned that this is critical whether you're in a startup or with a large multinational firm. Client conventions, industry trade shows, and external trainings are all good ways to get re-inspired while keeping up with trends and ideas.

7. Schedule a lunch or coffee at least once a week with inspired and inspiring people inside and outside of your organization: even though you're busy, make time to get a cup of coffee with the eager beaver fresh out of business school. You have a wealth of experience to share with them and they give you that fresh new perspective that you don't even realize you need. By the same token, take the initiative and schedule time with colleagues and mentors who think big and motivate you. My good friend Sandhya Devanathan is Head of Retail Products at Standard Chartered Singapore and she is one of the busiest people I know. Yet, somehow she makes time once a week to meet and connect with mentees and mentors inside and outside of her firm.

8. Maintain a social media presence: even if you don't want to put your life on Facebook, make a point to connect with people on LinkedIn. In this day and age, with everyone moving companies so often, it's the best way to stay in touch with your professional network. There are also great connections to be made on Twitter. That's how I met Susie Orman Schnall, author of *On Grace* and *The Balance Project: A Novel*. I was still relatively new to Twitter and I remember how excited I was to find a tweet from Susie inviting me to be part of The Balance Project, a popular interview series about the tragically glorified "doing it all" craze featuring inspiring and accomplished women including Reese Witherspoon and Molly Sims.

9. Keep your biography and resumé updated: I knew I was in a good place when people started asking for my bio and resumé and I could send them instantly. This meant that

others were asking for it as well. I was getting out there, and getting known. When someone asks for your resumé and it feels like a daunting project, it's a wakeup call.

10. Interview: people often ask me to interview potential candidates. Sometimes it can feel like a chore when I have a laundry list of to-dos. But then I remember that each interview is an opportunity to do market research. Or, as my friend Christine Amour-Levar encouragingly puts it, "Every conversation is a chance to discover something new." Similarly, going on interviews is an opportunity to learn and understand your worth.

I'm not naïve enough to think everything on this list will work for everyone. People are motivated and inspired by different things. I've been made much aware of this fact since meeting my husband. Case in point: the red umbrella pin.

As part of my six-month Citibank training in Miami, my

Promoting our customer promises

job was to spend time in different roles across various branches so I could understand all the details behind the retail bank operation: how to ensure there is adequate cash for each of the tellers and ATMs, how to adequately staff a branch to meet customers' needs, how to tally accounts to ensure there are no discrepancies within the tellers' rolls, and how to forward the cash to the bank's vaults if necessary. One week I was acting as a teller in Doral, the next I was shadowing a Personal Banker in South Beach, and months later I was covering as Assistant Branch Manager in Boca Raton. For the most part, the branch staff were warm and welcoming though frequently they would tease and call me "the mole."

When I was working in the branches, I would wear this red umbrella pin. A few years earlier, in what was then the largest corporate marriage in history, Citicorp had merged with financial conglomerate Travelers Group, creating a $155 billion global powerhouse. The Travelers' red umbrella became the bank's

Sandhya and I attending a MasterCard Innovation Forum 2014 with telecom engineer inventor and policymaker Sam Pitroda and former Asia Pacific President of MasterCard Vicky Bindra

official logo and it was quickly placed on everything from note-books and mouse pads to neckties and doorknobs. And of course, it was made into lapel pins. I initially put it on because, as a temporary trainee, I didn't have a nametag and I wanted customers to know I was part of the bank staff. I didn't realize it at the time but to many people at the branches the red umbrella pin signified importance. I was "management." On more than a few occasions, my colleagues in the branch asked me if I could get them one.

"Hi Claire, how's your morning going?" I remember one of the tellers, Gabriel, coming up to me while I was behind the window. Gabe was smart, driven, and cute. A Cuban-American Channing Tatum, if you will.

"Great," I answered as I continued to enter my last client's details into the system. I turned around to face him when I realized he was sticking around.

"How's everything with you?" I asked. This didn't feel like simple pleasantries.

"Good," he pulled over one of the stools after making sure no one was on line. "Hey, I wanted to ask you something," he said in a low voice.

Oh no, he's going to ask me out. He's far too young. It's going to be awkward and I'm supposed to be in this branch for another month.

As I was coming up with the best excuse to turn him down, he continued. "Is there any chance you might be able to get me one of those?" He pointed to my chest area, which took me aback for a moment until I realized he was pointing to the red umbrella pin.

I smiled, partly because of the small request and partly because of my big ego. I actually had a stash of these tucked away in my desk drawer. As part of the Management Associate program, we got a lot of Citi tchotchkes and, while many peers didn't pay them much mind, I saved everything (#dontforgetthesoap). Citi pens, calculators, mugs, tote bags, lawn chairs, mirrors—you name it, it's in my apartment somewhere.

Once I saw the value of these umbrella pins, I decided to use them as incentives. During the next morning branch huddle, I announced that whoever made a quality cross-sell referral that day would get a red umbrella pin. The response was overwhelming and I had to get my hands on more pins.

A few years later, Citi decided to spin off Travelers and focus on its main banking unit. Shortly after, we announced a new corporate logo. Essentially, the Travelers umbrella was transformed into an arc. The company welcomed the new identity with enthusiasm, and the new logo and identity implementations were underway. One morning, I walked into my office and found a white box sitting on my desk. I opened it to find a Citi arc pin complete with a brief story behind the new logo. As someone with an affinity for branding, I fully appreciated this internal awareness effort, but when I met Alex for coffee that morning I realized not everyone did.

"Hey, so did you see those pins sitting on our desks?" he asked casually as he stirred his Starbucks venti coffee. "How much do you think we spend on those things?" Alex works in Corporate Treasury so let's just say he doesn't always share my soft spot for all things marketing.

"Sure, there's some money involved, but changing a corporate identity is a big deal so it's built into expenses," I explained as we walked back to the office.

"But who cares about a little pin? They're just going to sit in everyone's drawer."

I laughed, "You're so wrong …" He obviously hadn't spent time in the branches.

When I got back up to my desk I had two emails from former colleagues in Miami. One read:

Hi Claire,

Hope this note finds you well.

I heard some people in New York received new Citi pins today. If you can manage to send some down, that would be great. We will wear them with pride here.

Of course, I forwarded these emails to my skeptical future husband right away.

When we first started dating in Sao Paulo

Future leaders

Promoting Global Client Banking at the flagship Mong Kok branch in Hong Kong

After giving the keynote speech at Citi's International Women's Day client event in 2013 with Head of ASEAN Michael Zink and Managing Director Julia Raiskin

DWYL

"Do what you love" (DWYL) has become the unofficial work mantra for our time. It has been considered the opposite of the monotonous corporate job. Between Steve Jobs, Oprah, and every speaker who delivers a commencement speech, doing what you love is the only way to live.

Most people who DWYL have an integrated life. They don't consider work to be work because they love what they do. What they do professionally is what they care about personally. Most people who DWYL also tend to have a little extra money. They're not necessarily multi-millionaires but their lifestyle may be partly subsidized by a trust fund, their spouse may earn enough so they can pursue their passion, or they may know that one day they'll inherit a $3 million dollar apartment that their parents bought for a fraction of that amount decades ago.

There was a wonderfully provoking piece about DWYL written by Miya Tokumitsu for *Slate*.[10] In the article, she submits

---

[10] Miya Tokumitsku, "In the Name of Love"

the "Do what you love" mantra that elites embrace actually devalues work and hurts workers. In doing so, she underlines the idea that DWYL is for the privileged few with wealth, social status, education, and political clout. Tokumitsu writes, "DWYL is a secret handshake of the privileged and a worldview that disguises its elitism as noble self-betterment."

While DWYL is a lovely idea, it's just not something most people have the luxury to do. But alas, instead of finding a job you love, you can learn to find meaning and success in the job you have. I want to share a few attitudinal tips that have helped me find my balance and DWYL in spite of (and sometimes even because of) my corporate job.

Live a Life of Purpose

One of the first things that struck me about Alex was that he was the first person I knew (aside from my very practical parents) who didn't buy into DWYL. "No, you don't need to do what you love; you just need to have a purpose," I remember him arguing over *caipirinhas* at Posto Seis, one of our favorite restaurants in Sao Paulo.

Alex grew up in a small town in upstate New York. To paint the picture of just how tiny of a town, he often tells the story about how his zip code changed after their postman retired. He and his three siblings could run around acres of land, they recognized every car that passed them by, and they were on a first name basis with everyone at the grocery store. While it was a wonderful place to grow up, he was always looking forward to moving to the city when he got older. He aspired to one day work on Wall Street, build a successful career, and have a big family. No one he knew from back home took this path so he never had one to follow.

When he visited the West Point Military Academy, however, he saw how much it had to offer by way of exposure and access. He made it a personal goal to get accepted to the prestigious academy and he achieved it. Anyone who knows my husband well

Alex participating in "lightning boot camp" alongside actors Ben Affleck and Josh Hartnett as part of their training for 2001 film *Pearl Harbor*

With platoon members in the 1-62 Air Defense Artillery: 25th Infantry Division Hawaii knows that he would be an unlikely fit at West Point. He never liked being told what to do, he would often challenge authority, and he was not exactly clean cut. But my husband can do anything when he knows it's for a greater purpose.

Today, Alex is the regional treasurer of Citi's broker dealer business in Asia. He's great at his job but I don't know if he would classify it as doing what he loves. At least for him, equally important as loving your job is loving the impact your job has on others. This can mean the internal clients who benefit from the work his team is doing or it can refer to the family he is able to help support.

My parents have a similar point of view. As new immigrants, they weren't necessarily doing what they loved but they were doing great work and living a meaningful life. Their jobs supported our family, allowing us to spend time together and providing us with opportunities to give back to the community.

Sometimes you have to do things you don't want to do. My kids have to perform for guests, my husband has to go to church, and I have to wake up in the wee hours. A little sacrifice makes you a better person. Chances are you'll never love 100 percent of your job. Even when I speak to people who are DWYL they still confess there's a portion of what they do that they don't enjoy in the least. Tracie Pang, who runs Singapore's Pangdemonium Theater, doesn't like fundraising. I haven't met her but I'm sure Kristen Stewart hates doing interviews. I don't love the evening calls associated with my job. Even if you can get to the point where you love 60 percent of what you do and find purpose in the other 40 percent, then you're golden.

Do Something for Yourself Each Day

I bookmarked a great list I came across a few months back called, "How to Make Your Life Better by Sending Five Simple Emails" by Eric Barker. The five emails were as follows:

1. Happiness: Every morning, send a friend, family member, or co-worker an email to say thanks for something.

Celebrating International Women's Day 2015

Singapore Council of Women's Organisation
Friday, 27th March 2015 at the Fullerton Hotel @ 7 pm

Each year in March, we celebrate International Women's Day (IWD) which is designated by the United Nations as a special day to provide an opportunity to reflect on the advancements made by women, to consider the challenges faced today, and to assess our role in the future.

Citi Women and supporters celebrating International Women's Day in Singapore

Attending the FWN Filipina Leadership Global Summit 2014 in Manila. From left to right: Former Secretary of Foreign Affairs Delia Albert, me, businesswoman and philanthropist Loida Nicolas Lewis, my fabulous Filipina mother, Citi Consumer Business Manager Bea Teh-Tan

2. Job: At the end of the week, send your boss an email and sum up what you've accomplished.
3. Growth: Once a week, email a potential mentor.
4. Friendship: Email a good friend and make plans.
5. Career: Send an email to someone you know (but don't know very well) and check in.

The point is that you carve out time to do something for your own betterment. This is easy to overlook when you have mountains of tasks in front of you, but invest this little time in yourself and everything else actually gets easier.

Think Fulfillment and Integration Over Having it All[11]

Not everyone can quit their job to pursue their passion. Most of us have to find ways to integrate the two. For me, one definition of success is achieving an integrated life. Writing my books has allowed me to integrate my personal and professional life, essentially simulating DWYL. My books have added these other dimensions to my life:

- I have established my personal brand and platform to share what matters most to me;
- I picked up what often feels like another master's degree, this time in social media;
- I have broadened my everyday world outside of my industry. This has allowed me to be better at my job;
- They've helped me to minimize the importance of corporate politics and hierarchy;
- They allowed me to connect with so many interesting people around the world about their families, their careers, and their dreams.

However, long before I had written a book, I was also

---

[11] "A New Vocabulary: Fulfillment and Integration over 'Having It All'" was the name of the insightful panel session at Claudia Chan's 3rd Annual S.H.E. Summit: The Global Leadership & Lifestyle Event.

Meeting some of my readers in Vancouver

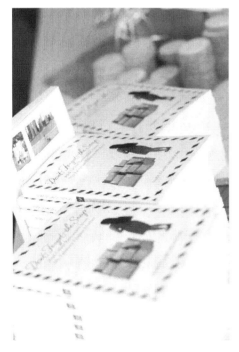

Book display at the Philipine Center in New York City

With Philippine Ambassador to Singapore Antonio A. Morales

pursuing this integration. I had a great job that I was enjoying but I still had other interests, so I looked for opportunities to get involved in different areas of the bank where I could pursue them. As my friend Claudia says, "Even in a job you enjoy, you never fully utilize all your talents or fulfill all of your interests so it's important to have other outlets."

One advantage of working for a large company is that somewhere in the organization there is a group focused on something near to your heart. No matter what your passion is, some part of the firm is doing it. Diversity—there's a whole department for that. Non-profit work—there's a foundation dedicated to enriching communities. Education—you bet. Big organizations sponsor so many worthy causes, be it Habitat for Humanity, March of Dimes, or The Junior League. There is always a corporate table that needs to be filled. Ask anyone in Corporate Affairs. They are often scrambling to find people in the business who can attend.

My world opened up when I connected to Citi Community Relations. All it took was one email saying how I was interested in our Habitat for Humanity efforts and soon I was on the distribution list for all related events. I remember how thrilled I was to receive my first invite from Dana Deubert, Head of Corporate Communications. I still have her amusing response to my thank you email, "Here's to many more nights of rubber chicken!" Nothing could have made me happier.

Don't Let Perfection Hold You Back

As I was writing my first book, I thought my mother was crazy when she asked if I'd be ready to publish it a few short months later. She was reading through my first draft and said, "This is it already. You just need to have it professionally edited." She proceeded to draft a timeline. Two weeks for copy editing, two weeks for book layout, two weeks for back and forth changes, two weeks for printing, and *voilà*.

"I won't be ready. I may still want to add a few more chap-

Waiting in the green room before our joint TV interview

ters about our move to Singapore. I was also considering a recipe section ..." I rationalized.

"Save it for the next one. If you don't stick to a deadline, you'll never be done. If you wait for it to be perfect, you'll never finish the book," she said matter-of-factly.

She was right. I've come across so many people who tell me that they once started a book and never finished it. I know I'm no better than them but they didn't have my mother. Around the same time, I was reading *Lean In* by Sheryl Sandberg where she poignantly stated, "Done is better than perfect."[12] I couldn't agree more.

Succeed on Your Own Terms

While I was working in New York, the general counsel for my business, Neil Barry, coined me the nickname Sunshine. "You're just always so upbeat and happy," he explained genuinely.

---

[12] Sheryl Sandberg, *Lean In: Women, Work, and the Will to Lead*

So I've heard. Upbeat and happy were fine traits and all, but "Sunshine" was not the nickname I wanted as I was working my way up the corporate ladder. It doesn't exactly give off a "serious business woman" vibe.

Since then, I've come to realize, "So what?" I generally have a cheerful disposition but that doesn't stop me from being great at what I do. It may actually be part of what makes me effective at what I do. As cliché as it may sound, Judy Garland's advice has come to resonate with me now more than ever: "Always be a first-rate version of yourself, instead of a second-rate version of somebody else."

Similarly, you have to make your own rules. When I was first considering a job in Singapore, many people warned me that I wouldn't be able to see my kids during the week. "They work late in Asia," it is commonly known. This turned out to be true but I'm glad it didn't dissuade me from making the move. When I first got to Singapore, I followed what seemed to be the default schedule, which meant a later start to what I was used to in New York and a later end. Not only did I find myself staying late in the office but when I got home, because I was managing the Global Client business, I was also on evening calls with New York. After a few months I realized I needed to adjust my schedule to make time for family.

When you're a professional, you know what you need to do to get the job done. Being at the office when my kids were having dinner and going to bed was not required to get the job done. I made a schedule that worked for me and it had no negative impact on my boss or my team. I came to the office early and got home in time to have dinner with my kids, and then I went back online to answer emails and take calls after my kids went to bed. Had I listened to all the people telling me not to take this job while my kids were young, I would have missed out on an incredible opportunity to work in Asia.

So honored to be associated with these inspiring Filipina women leaders

Speaking at a luncheon hosted by Financial Women's Association of Singapore

Launching *Don't Forget the Soap* at Fully Booked in Manila

With my mother at APEC 2015

Taking Carlos and Isabel to their first day of school in Hong Kong

With Consul General Vic Dimagiba and Consul Mersole Mellejor at the Philippine Embassy in Singapore

Sharing stories from *Don't Forget the Soap* at Fully Booked in Manila

With Citi Women colleagues in the Philippines

Enjoying last day of maternity leave with my babies

Morning skype when Alex was working out of Hong Kong while we were still in Singapore

Alex and his family with some of my closest friends during one of his business trips back to New York

With fashion designer, business woman and philanthropist Tory Burch at the opening of her flagship store in Singapore

Alex joining me on a Citi Women panel to discuss the role of men in supporting women's leadership

Protesting Philippine political corruption from New York City

With my two girls

Other Reflections

My dear friend May and her husband Marcel supporting my mother during
her New York solo exhibit at Tally Beck Contemporary in 2013

WOULD YOU SERVE DRINKS
AT MY MOTHER'S ART SHOW?

*"True friendship isn't about being there when it's convenient,
it's about being there when it's not."* — Unknown

OTIVATIONAL SPEAKER JIM ROHN SAYS
that we are the average of the five people we spend the most time
with. According to him, when it comes to relationships we are
greatly influenced—whether we like it or not—by those closest to
us. These five people affect our way of thinking, our self-esteem,
and our decisions. Of course, everyone is their own person, but research shows that our environment affects us more than we think.
If this is the case, then between my family and friends I really did
win Lotto 6/49. I have great friends. I know everyone says that,
but I really do. I've actually had people ask me, "How do you have
so many quality friendships?"

　　If there's one thing I don't mind sounding braggy about,
it's the good friends I've made everywhere I've lived: Vancouver,
New York City, Seville, Miami, Sao Paulo, Manila, Singapore, and
most recently Hong Kong. Alex always says I get this from my

mother and he's probably right. She has dozens of long standing friendships that have stood the test of time. I have no doubt mine will be the same.

My litmus test for friendship has always been, "Would they serve drinks at my mom's art show?" From early on, I was conscious of the difference between real friends and capricious friends (my father would call them "fair-weather" friends). To this day, I still tease my real friend May about being in the fair-weather friend category for the first two years after we met. As I relayed in my first book, the only reason May first took an interest in me was because she learned that her high school crush BJ Centenera was a close family friend.

My mother's career as an artist officially began when I was in high school. She had always found ways to incorporate art into our lives but she only began working on her own pieces again in New York. Every night after dinner she went off to the studio at the School of Visual Arts. I'm sure this had to be exhausting after teaching five-year-old kids all day but she was motivated and inspired. Her hard work paid off because not even two years later she began holding solo exhibits in New York City.

You would think a solo exhibit would be daunting, especially one where the guest of honor was Agnes Gund, President of the Museum of Modern Art. Not for my mother. She and my father had events down pat. Whether it was a dinner party with fifty of our closest friends (this was about the size of our "small" dinner parties while growing up in the Filipino community) or a fundraising event with hundreds of attendees, my parents were never fazed. Years later when people would ask how we were all so stress-free and calm during my wedding in Manila, I had to explain that the affair was on the small-medium end of events my parents have hosted (we had 200 guests).

Back in Vancouver, my parents hosted events on a monthly basis. They could be anything from church fundraisers at All Saints Parish Hall to Filipino choral groups at the big downtown theater in Robson Square. The Madrigal Singers is the name of the main choral group from the University of the Philippines. Anyone familiar with Filipinos knows that Filipinos are some of the world's best singers. I'm not kidding. From cruise ships and hotel lounges around the world, to *American Idol* and Any Country's *Got Talent*, Filipinos are represented in disproportionately large numbers. My parents would organize performances to showcase Filipino artists and help them get exposure in Canada. They would fundraise to secure the venue or they would get their friends to house the talent. Justin and I became accustomed to waking up and finding ourselves eating breakfast with concert pianist Raul Sunico, Madrigal singers, and *Bayanihan* dancers.

Ten years later, art shows were a breeze for my mother. At least as far as the event planning goes. She had her network of people to help put up the works, promote the event, and prepare the food (wine and cheese don't cut it at the Philippine Consulate). She would then not so subtly ask if any of my friends "might like" to come to the opening reception and maybe help serve drinks. I was fourteen and had just regained confidence after moving from the suburbs of Vancouver to New York City. I wasn't spending recess in the bathroom stall anymore and I had gotten over any intimidation I had with the cool kids, but asking them to work an art show at the Philippine Center? That was a little bit of a stretch.

There were boatloads of people I could invite to, say, my birthday party but only a handful of them I would be comfortable asking to come and serve drinks at my mother's art show. That's when I realized that it was those people who were my real friends; everyone else was an acquaintance. People often think it's easy to tell the difference between the two but many still confuse them. Maybe that's because "acquaintance" always sounds like someone you may have met once or twice but they're often actually people you see every day. You spend time together because of common or convenient circumstances. But real friends aren't just there when it's convenient; they're there when it's not. I've since come to learn that the people who will serve drinks at my mother's art show are the same people who will be there for me when I'm sick, when I'm heartbroken, when I need inspiration, and when I need to veg out.

From then on, whenever I move to a new city and meet new people, I always size them up by seeing if I can picture them serving drinks at my mother's next art show. Whether meeting people as a student, as a young professional, or as an executive, this litmus test has always helped me make meaningful connections and friendships. I've met some highly impressive people while moving around the last several years. Some run large businesses, some are successful entrepreneurs, and some fundraise for humanitarian causes. I am grateful to be surrounded by so many people who dream big and motivate others. Still, if I can't see them serving drinks at my mother's art show, then they remain an acquaintance, maybe even an inspiration, but not a true friend.

Times I Know I am Being Irrational

Another great thing about true friends is that they accept everything about you, including irrational behavior.

Alex and Carlos surprising me at the airport

Some of our closest friends from Singapore visiting us in Hong Kong

Carlos surprising best buddy Nico and his family at the airport

Henny (my childhood best friend) and Kristen (my college best friend) having a laugh over their stories in my book

With some of my closest girlfriends in Singapore during my third baby shower

Childhood cousins and friends reunited in Vancouver

Cats

I have an irrational fear of cats. I used to be pretty good at hiding this fact, especially when I would show up at someone's apartment and realize they have one. I would squirm on the inside and lift my legs the whole time under the table, but no one would know. Now, whenever we arrive at a home with a feline in residence, Alex announces to the hosts, "She's terrified of cats." The first time he did this, I kicked him under the table but he rightly pointed out that this way I can relax and have a good time, plus he wouldn't have to sit through dinner with my fingernails dug into his arm.

Morning-After Notes

Back in the day, when my girlfriends would stay over in my New York studio we would have the best time. I was always out the door first in the morning since I had the most traditional corporate job. When I got home in the evening, a part of me would be disappointed if I didn't find a note left for me on the dining table. I wasn't expecting a long love letter or anything, just a simple "Had a great time as always! Xoxo"

Airport Pick Ups

No matter how much time I spend there, something about being at the airport—any airport—is still exciting to me. I love seeing families reunited as I wait for my parents to get through immigration and I feel teary eyed when I see loved ones stalling their goodbyes as I make my way through security. Even when I'm traveling for business, I find myself smiling as I walk out of baggage claim. I know it's silly but part of me always thinks someone I know may surprise me at the airport.

FOMO

I never knew the term for it before but I have always had a moderate case of FOMO (fear of missing out). Nothing makes me happier than integrating friendships, but once those friends start making plans on their own I feel a little sad. At the very least, I want ongoing credit for the fact that I introduced them.

Soon after I moved to Asia, my brother Justin suddenly starting making a bunch of new friends in New York. It started out innocently enough. A couple people I didn't recognize here, a few new faces there. But soon it started getting a little out of control as far as I was concerned. At one point Justin had even created a hashtag counting down the days until someone's visit. I found myself irrationally livid. *Who are these people? Why don't I know them? Are you doing a countdown for me this summer?* I knew I had to get it together when Justin calmly said that he was considering posting with Facebook's "show everyone except" button. Since then, I've spent time with his friends and they are the loveliest people.

Grudges

I hold grudges for far too long. Alex always says that if I remember something he did to upset me ten years ago, we can be transported back to 2005. It's one thing for your husband to say this, but when all your friends say the same it may be a problem. My friends Sheldon, Danny, and Khamen often joke about my "Tuesday morning emails." They might say something in passing at dinner on Friday night but I would let it simmer until Tuesday morning, by which point I would have gathered my thoughts enough to write a three-page email outlining all the reasons they disappointed me. Only true friends put up with it.

Breakfast in the Hamptons with some of my closest college friends

Goodbye drinks with Singapore girlfriends before moving to Hong Kong.
From left to right: Margarita Locsin Chan, Amanda Griffin Jacob, me, Claudia Curran,
Christine Amour-Levar, Yasmin Schleider

A recent group exhibit organized by my mother to promote Vancouver based Filipino artists.
Front row left to right: my mother, Philippine Ambassador to Canada Petronila Garcia,
Consul General Neil Ferrer

My mother being interviewed during her 2011 exhibit at
Cultural Center of the Philippines

My friends supporting my mother during her
group show at Di Legno Gallery in Singapore

Actress and Yale classmate Kellie Martin and
her mother attending my mom's art show
at the Philippine Center in New York back
in 1996

Some of our closest and dearest friends at our wedding
rehearsal dinner in Manila

The Bayanihan Dance Company show my parents organized in Vancouver

With my Spanish "sister" Myriam during junior study abroad in Seville

Cathching up with some of our closest friends while on a recent business trip to Singapore

Ladies catch up dinner

Bringing friends to see my mother's work at Affordable Art Fair Singapore

Central Park picnic with some of our closest friends in New York

Former colleagues turned great friends

Midnight Anxieties

It goes without saying that I'm a generally happy person. But since we're on confessions, I thought I'd share some of my other anxieties. In her new book, *Why Not Me?* Mindy Kaling shared a list of things that wake her up at 4:00 a.m. I liked this idea so I'm going to do the same. While admittedly nothing wakes me up at 4:00 a.m. these are things that keep me up at midnight. Some self-indulgent, some selfless, all real.

1. Did I leave the aircon on in the living room?
2. Will Alex get upset about the electricity bill this month?
3. Did I transfer money for school payments?
4. Does Carlos have homework I was supposed to review for tomorrow? Does Isa have show and tell tomorrow? Do I spend as much time with Isa as I did with Carlos at this age?
5. What am I going to do when Sofia's in school? I can't believe she's almost one. Hey, why doesn't she have any teeth yet?
6. That reminds me, I haven't found a dentist in Hong Kong.
7. Is my team back in Singapore happy?
8. Is my new boss in New York happy?
9. When should I be going for that next job?
10. If Fintech really takes off, could we all be out of jobs? I need to tell Justin and his friends to stop using Venmo.
11. Since Justin and his friends are running the NYC marathon, should I? Maybe for my fortieth birthday next year.
12. I'm almost forty. I just have one year left to qualify for "40 under 40" lists.
13. How can I get Alex's family here for his fortieth birthday?
14. Will he ever resent me for living outside the US for this long?

15. How long will my parents be able to travel this much? They're almost seventy.

16. Then again, so is Hillary Clinton. Am I doing enough for Americans Abroad for Hillary?

17. How do I get to a White House Correspondents' Dinner? If Jessica Simpson gets to go, why shouldn't I?

18. Do I post too much on social media?

19. What if people think my second book isn't as good as my first one?

20. When will these baby hairs go away?

21. Will I ever have a flat tummy again?

22. What if we can't recreate our Singapore social circle in Hong Kong?

23. What if we never end up living in the same city as my closest friends and our kids never get to be best friends?

24. What if my kids are spoiled?

25. What if my parents aren't around to help me un-spoil them?

Then, I try to remember all the perspective my parents give me. I count my blessings, say fifty Hail Marys, and fall asleep.

Three children at play

Sweet and happy Isabel

Reunion with close family in Canada

Pulling off Alex's 40th birthday surprise with the Moore family on a recent trip to New York

Visiting Kristen in San Francisco

New Year's Eve 2014

The kids with some of their closest pals in Singapore

With Kristen's daughter Kaya

Three generations

Carlos and Isabel at ages 5 and 3

Carlos, Isabel and Sofia in Boracay

Oops, I Forgot the Soap

ONE THING I'VE HAD TO ADMIT TO MYSELF is that no matter how much I like to think I'm grounded, having had the immigrant experience and all, there are times I still forget the soap—literally and figuratively.[13]

A few months ago I flew to the Philippines to attend the Filipina Women's Network Global100 Summit. I was eight months pregnant (I just barely made it on the plane) and I was exhausted after finishing a big presentation at work, running home to spend time with kids, and then rushing to make my flight. All I wanted to do was pass out when I got to my seat but I couldn't get comfortable in my aisle seat until Middle Seat and Window Seat were settled. Once that happened, I took comfort in knowing I could get some shuteye. The only good thing about flying a discount airline is that no one will wake you to eat since you don't get a meal. Every other time except this one, anyway. Just as I was falling into REM sleep, the flight attendant tapped my arm.

---

[13] My friend and colleague, Jerry Blanton, once teased over drinks, "Hey, I have an idea. Your next book should be called, 'Oops, I Forgot the Soap!'" Little did he know this would stick.

"Excuse me, Mrs. Moore ..." she said gently.

I reluctantly opened my eyes, "Yes?" I like to think I still sounded polite at this point.

"You selected the Plus bundle when you purchased your seat and this entitles you to food and beverage vouchers," she explained.

"Oh, okay," I was still in a daze. And now I was conflicted. Sleep vs. snack. I never turn down food so I pulled out the laminated menu from the seat pocket in front of me. "I'll do the cupcake and juice combo." I had managed to make a quick stop by McDonald's (surprise) before entering the Departures gate so, if anything, dessert was in order. A little irritated that I wasn't asleep yet, I flipped through Jetstar's magazine while I waited for my complimentary snack, which seemed to take forever, of course.

The cupcake arrived (to my surprise, it was a fancy looking chocolate cupcake from the Singapore-based chain Twelve Cupcakes) but now I was annoyed with myself for choosing orange juice. There was a 50 percent chance the cupcake would be chocolate and everyone knows orange juice never goes with chocolate. My sleep deprivation had clearly led to bad judgment. Still, I managed to enjoy the chocolate cupcake, which was delightfully moist and delicious. I saved the clashing juice for later. Now it was finally time to sleep. I pulled out my pashmina to use as a blanket and I got comfortable. Well, as comfortable as you can get in Jetstar Economy.

But, just as I started drifting away again, I heard the same flight attendant's voice. "Excuse me, Mrs. Moore?"

"What is it?" I asked, this time not as sweetly.

"When you order the cupcake combo, it entitles you to a free entry in our raffle," she explained, holding a piece of paper and a pen.

"I'm fine. I don't need to enter, thanks," I said as I not-so-subtly shifted my body away from the aisle.

"You could win a free trip to anywhere that Jetstar goes," she continued with enthusiasm. Was she purposely torturing me?

"I'm okay," I managed a fake smile and this time closed my eyes.

"You could go to Australia, New Zealand—"

"I'm sorry," I felt justified cutting her off at this point. "I really just need to sleep." As soon as I heard myself, I regretted snapping at her.

"Oh," she looked down, slightly dejected, "I thought you might be interested in the free trip. I guess you don't need it ..." She started to walk back down the aisle. I was a horrible person.

"Excuse me," I called her back, "I changed my mind. Of course, I would love to do the raffle."

She smiled genuinely as she handed me the form. "If you win, you could give the free trip to one of your relatives."

I never got to sleep for the rest of the trip but I'm still grateful to the flight attendant for waking me up.

In all likelihood, there will be times when I forget the soap and my kids will continue having the expat experience rather than the immigrant experience. Still, it's nice to know that some positively Filipino traits have inevitably been passed down.

The other day, we were in the Philippines sitting in traffic. In Manila, it's not uncommon for what's usually a thirty-minute drive to take over three hours.

"Ugh, I can't believe it's taking this long," I complained, restless.

"But sometimes it's nice to have traffic," Carlos said from the backseat.

This alone stopped my grumbling. I laughed and asked, "Why is it nice?"

Without skipping a beat, he answered, "More time with the family."

Reunion with closest relatives in the Philippines

At the airport with nannies (and sisters) Richel and Regina who provide us with wonderful support

Like twins sometimes

Picking up *Lolo* from the airport

ACKNOWLEDGEMENTS

*T*HANK YOU TO MY POSITIVELY FILIPINO FAMILY FOR CREATING MORE MEMORIES THAN OUR HEARTS CAN HOLD. My parents, Jose and Lenore, for being unfailingly positive yet sensibly realistic, and for continuing to guide me in making purposeful decisions. My honorary Filipino husband, Alex, for his generous spirit and unwavering strength, for lifting me up always, as well as grounding me sometimes. My brother, Justin, for the infectious laughs and social media counsel, and for being the brother everyone wishes they had. My three little loves, Carlos, Isabel, and Sofia, who give us all immeasurable joy, countless smiles, and boundless inspiration.

I am also grateful to my extended family and friends who continue to act as sounding boards and advisors: Clorinda Moore, Natasha Muslih, Jose Hunt, Angelica Kristen Jongco, Tanya Loh, Alexis Neophytides, Sandhya Devanathan, Julie Barry, and Christine Amour-Levar.

I would not have received all the opportunities that followed the launch of my first book launch if it weren't for Carissa Villacorta, Pauline Mangosing, Mina V. Esguerra, and Bituin Aquino. I hope we have many more projects ahead of us.

Sincerest thanks to Bennett R. Coles, Amy O'Hara, and everyone at Promontory Press. I am grateful to be working with such a wonderful team.

Deepest gratitude to my Citi colleagues and friends around the world for the overwhelming support.

Finally, a big thank you to Nonie Cartagena-dono for his talent and patience in once again designing every last inch of this book.

Lenore RS Lim
Layered Life C
Mixed Media, 2015
30" x 24"